LIVE LIKE FRANCIS

LIVE LIKE FRANCIS
....

Reflections on
Franciscan Life
in the World

Jovian Weigel, OFM
Leonard Foley, OFM

EDITED BY
Diane M. Houdek, OFS

Franciscan
MEDIA
Cincinnati, Ohio

Cover design by Candle Light Studios
Book design by Mark Sullivan

ISBN 978-1-61636-971-2

Printed in the United States of America.
Printed on acid-free paper.
16 17 18 19 20 5 4 3 2 1

CONTENTS

INTRODUCTION

....

"The Lord give you peace!"[1]

—St. Francis

A most beautiful quality of Francis was his courtesy. He welcomed all who came to him. And so we welcome you in your quest to discover his life and spirit in ways that may deepen and enliven your journey as a Christian.

Through the centuries, the Lord has gathered people together in the way of Francis. From the beginning, Francis had a vision for people living ordinary lives in the world but following the rule and example he laid out for the brothers living in community with him. That vision first evolved into the Third Order (also known as Secular Franciscans). Their rule, originating with Francis and updated most recently in 1978, can offer a helpful guide for people who want to live the Gospel according to the way of Francis in their own time and place.

In every age there are those who seek to live in the spirit in which Francis lived eight centuries ago. The heart of this book is the message of *The Third Order Vocation*, a book that caught the hearts of thousands of those who long to follow Francis when it first appeared some fifty years ago.

In 2001, that original small blue book was revised and published under the title *To Live as Francis Lived*. It retained the simplicity and the spirit of Franciscan living expressed by Franciscan Fathers Leonard Foley and Jovian Weigel while adding new material to harmonize the work with the Rule of the Secular Franciscan Order approved by Pope Paul VI in 1978. Many people have used *To Live as Francis Lived* as a way to begin to explore a call to living

Franciscan ideals in the midst of daily life. In this third iteration, we have tried to open this vision to people both in and beyond the Secular Franciscan community.

SUGGESTIONS ON HOW TO USE THIS BOOK

....

This book is divided into reflections that can be used to span a year by contemplating one aspect of the Franciscan way each week. Through these fifty-two reflections, you will learn about the Franciscan way of life.

After reading and reflecting on the topic, consider the "Questions for Reflection" at the end. This is not an examination but an opportunity for you to express yourself—where you are going, where you are growing.

"Connecting with Scripture" suggests a Scripture reading on the theme of the reflection. If you are serious about living the Gospel, you need to know what Jesus said and did. Francis received his guidance from the Spirit by taking the Word of God very seriously, reading it regularly. We must do the same so that it may make a home in us.

"Connecting with Franciscan Writings" features a brief passage by or about Francis, Clare, and the Franciscan way of life. We hope this will whet your appetite for further reading. A list of resources at the back of the book can give you some suggestions for doing just that.

Consider the "Application to Daily Life" suggestions faithfully, prayerfully, and honestly to see how Francis is affecting your life. The way of Francis is not so much a way of thinking, as it is a way of living. We should feel a sense of urgency in following the way of the Lord, yet at the same time remain people of peace and hope.

Each reflection concludes with a brief prayer. That prayer is designed to continue your own conversation or listening time with the Lord. Carry it in your heart and mind throughout the week.

It is best to set a regular day and time for study. Make a commitment to a duration that will help you stay disciplined and able to absorb the material. You might want to begin a journal as well, writing down insights the Holy Spirit sends you, prayers and thoughts that enlighten you. You will find that you progress a great deal, even though the growth may seem almost imperceptible at the time.

Also set aside regular time for prayer. Pray any way you wish: in your own words, using a prayer book, using Scripture, the rosary, or some form of the Liturgy of the Hours.

....

PART ONE

Foundation

The foundation of the Franciscan way of life is Jesus Christ and no other. To follow Francis's way is to strive with all our bodies, minds and spirits to go from "Gospel to life and life to the Gospel." To begin to accomplish that, we must know the Gospel of Jesus in order to live our lives in accord with it. To know the Gospel, we must know the Lord. That is the direction toward which each of the following reflections leads us. We who have followed Jesus now begin again to bring our lives into the Gospel life, the Gospel into our everyday lives.

....

Beginning Again

"Let us begin to do good, for as yet we have done
little."
— St. Francis of Assisi

Francis spoke these words at a time when most people already considered him a saint. In his mind, there was no plateau in life where he could feel he had "made it" and could coast into heaven from then on. He did not compare his love with that of other men but with that of Christ; hence, he always saw an infinite expanse into which he could still go, becoming more and more like his Lord.

God has already blessed you with his life and given you the gift of faith and faithfulness. Each time we begin anew, we enter a new phase of life intent on enriching our relationship with God. You are not entering upon something different from the Christian life or something better than the life of other Christians. You are looking, like Francis and with Francis, into that vast expanse of Christ's love, and you desire to share it more deeply. The only thing different about your new life is that your Christian life will now be given a particular coloring and direction by Francis and the traditions that have grown from his life and words. You're beginning again, and you will continue to begin again for the rest of your life.

We often think that God's call comes to us when we have achieved a level of spiritual perfection, when we are worthy of so great a calling. But the reality for most of us is that we get hints and suggestions of a new direction for our lives at the most unexpected (and occasionally inopportune) times. It was this way for Jesus's first apostles. And it was this way for Francis and many of the saints.

In your spiritual life, you must be satisfied to progress gradually. Usually you will not notice your growth. Sometimes it may even seem you are growing backward as you discover your weaknesses and failings. But trust in God. Allow God to lead you through your spiritual companions, through the reflections of this book, through your own study and prayer.

Week by week, you will turn your attention from one aspect of the spiritual life to another. It's like painting a picture: a touch here, a dab there, and gradually the masterpiece emerges. When you finish this year of reflection, study, and prayer, you will be just beginning a deeper and more fruitful life with God.

No deep understanding of Jesus, Francis, and Clare can be reached without God's direction through prayer. Make each action part of your prayer life. Invite the Holy Spirit to lead you not just to mental knowledge but to a deep spiritual understanding that will result in your conversion. Conversion is the ongoing process of learning to live the gospel way of life given to us by Jesus and revealed to us by Francis and Clare.

QUESTIONS FOR REFLECTION

- In what ways do you hope to deepen your love of God?
- What mistakes have you made in the past that have kept you from God?
- What attitude in you has been the greatest hindrance to deepening your love of God?
- Do you feel you can have a better spirit formed in you?

CONNECTING WITH SCRIPTURE

Once while Jesus was standing beside the lake of Gennesaret, and the crowd was pressing in on him to hear the word of God, he saw two boats there at the shore of the lake; the fishermen had gone out of them and were washing their nets. He got into one of the boats, the one belonging to Simon, and asked him to put out a little way from the shore. Then he sat down and taught the crowds from the boat. When he had finished speaking, he said to Simon, "Put out into the deep water and let down your nets for a catch." Simon answered, "Master, we have worked all night long but have caught nothing. Yet if you say so, I will let down the nets." When they had done this, they caught so many fish that their nets were beginning to break. So they signaled to their partners in the other boat to come and help them. And they came and filled both boats, so that they began to sink. But when Simon Peter saw it, he fell down at Jesus' knees, saying, "Go away from me, Lord, for I am a sinful man!" For he and all who were with him were amazed at the catch of fish that they had taken; and so also were James and John, sons of Zebedee, who were partners with Simon. Then Jesus said to Simon, "Do not be afraid; from now on you will be catching people." When they had brought their boats to shore, they left everything and followed him.

—Luke 5:1–11

CONNECTING WITH FRANCISCAN WRITINGS

Francis lifted his head from the stone floor and looked searchingly into the eyes of the crucifix that seemed now to have depth, like real eyes. Suddenly, the whole face of the Christ seemed to move, and Francis was afraid. Then as from some faraway place and yet coming surely from the crucifix, a voice clear and resonant pierced Francis' soul.

"Francis, go now and repair my church which, as you see, is falling down."

Francis was jubilant. He waited for more, and he searched and searched the face of the crucifix, but there was no movement, no sign that more would come. Francis remained transfixed for a long time, and thanked Jesus over and over again for this clear request He had made of him. He would start rebuilding the church immediately.

It never occurred to Francis that Christ was asking anything other than the actual repairing of churches that were falling into ruin. So he ran from San Damiano and set about collecting stones to rebuild crumbling churches. He would start with San Damiano itself. His whole mind and energy were now focused almost fanatically on this one project.

This single-minded obedience to his dreams and voices was to become a bold pattern in Francis' life that would lead to his total and radical service of the gospel of Christ.

—Murray Bodo, *Francis: The Journey and the Dream*

APPLICATION TO DAILY LIFE

- Experiment this week with the best time—and length of time—to reflect, study, and pray each day. Make your plan realistic—don't try to do too much.

PRAYER

Lord, you promise to make all things new.
That includes me.
As I begin this journey
to discover St. Francis's way to you,
I ask you to begin to renew
my faith, my hope, and my love.
Amen.

Franciscan Life in the World

"The Franciscan family, as one among many
spiritual families raised up by the Holy Spirit
in the Church, unites all members of the People
of God—laity, religious, and priests—who
recognize that they are called to follow Christ in
the footsteps of St. Francis of Assisi.

In various ways and forms but in life-giving
union with each other, they intend to make
present the charism of their common Seraphic
Father in the life and mission of the Church."

—Rule of the Secular Franciscan Order, 1

Francis simply wanted to follow the Gospel literally,
wholeheartedly, and humbly. Others were inspired by his
example and captured by his vision. In a comparatively short
time, the little group of Franciscans grew into an order of
thousands that needed organization. Francis was careful to have
every development of the Order approved by the Holy Father. The
original Rule, a collection of Gospel texts, was expanded over
time and became the final and definitive Rule of 1223 which First
Order Franciscans still observe today.

On one of his wanderings, Francis met a merchant named
Luchesio in the town of Poggibonsi. Luchesio had been a rather
hard man who watched his money very carefully, though he was
strangely generous to the poor, gave lodging to pilgrims, and helped
widows and orphans. Francis seems to have had no influence in
his conversion but gave him and his wife, Bona Donna, a norm of

life. After this, Luchesio devoted all his time to works of charity, especially care of the sick in hospitals. He wore a rough tunic of a simple peasant with a rope around his waist. When he was home, he worked in a little garden he had retained after parting with his other possessions, and he sold the produce from it. If this way of life did not bring him enough, he would go out and beg.

A number of people with the same spirit gathered around Luchesio. Francis gave a rule of life to these followers (later called the Brothers and Sisters of Penance, which means those who turn to God from a sinful and idle life). They sought to imitate in the world the ways of Francis and his brothers. As soon as they entered the brotherhood, they pledged themselves to give back all unjustly acquired goods—which in many cases meant to give up everything—to pay the tithes which they might owe, to make their wills in time to prevent strife among their heirs, to not bear arms, to not take an oath except in special extraordinary cases, and to not accept public office. They wore a poor and distinctive habit and divided their time between prayer and deeds of charity. They generally lived with their families, but sometimes, like the Friars Minor, they withdrew into solitude.

Around 1221, Cardinal Hugolino and Francis wrote the first formal Rule for the Third Order. We no longer have the original copy of this rule, but it was certainly the foundation of the Rule of 1228, which we do have. For nearly eight centuries, this gathering of the faithful has been striving to live the Gospel life in the world under the direction of the Franciscan Order and according to the Rule of Francis as approved and adapted by the Church.

The Order has had its ups and downs. There have been periods of great spiritual fervor and also times when the vision of Francis was somewhat eclipsed. Today there are three branches of what is called the First Order of St. Francis: the Friars Minor (OFM), the

Capuchins (OFM Cap.) and the Conventuals (OFM Conv.). When St. Clare and other women followed the example of Francis, the Second Order was founded, known today as the Poor Clares.

Some members of the Third Order band together to live in community, take the three vows of poverty, chastity, and obedience, and observe a rule approved by the Holy See. They are called Third Order "Regulars" (TOR) and comprise most of the Franciscan sisters with whom you may be familiar. The Third Order Secular, now known as the Secular Franciscan Order, consists of Franciscans who live in the world and meet together in small groups known as fraternities.

QUESTIONS FOR REFLECTION

- What is your experience of formal religious orders? Have you ever felt called to life in a religious community?
- How might people living and working in secular (nonreligious) surroundings bring the vision of the Gospel to people in different ways than priests and religious professionals?

CONNECTING WITH SCRIPTURE

The next day John again was standing with two of his disciples, and as he watched Jesus walk by, he exclaimed, "Look, here is the Lamb of God!" The two disciples heard him say this, and they followed Jesus. When Jesus turned and saw them following, he said to them, "What are you looking for?" They said to him, "Rabbi" (which translated means Teacher), "where are you staying?" He said to them, "Come and see." They came and saw where he was staying, and they remained with him that day. It was about four o'clock in the afternoon. One of the two who heard John speak and followed him was Andrew, Simon Peter's brother. He first found his brother Simon and said to him, "We have found the Messiah" (which is translated Anointed). He brought Simon to Jesus, who looked at him and said, "You are Simon son of John. You are to be called Cephas" (which is translated Peter).

—John 1:35–42

CONNECTING WITH FRANCISCAN WRITINGS

Francis always thought of the early days of the brotherhood as the Rivotorto times. In those days the brothers all huddled together in a single sty through the heat of summer into the cold and wet autumn of winter's chills and into spring when the rains kept floors and walls constantly damp, and the whole interior was musty. Those were the happy times. It was so crowded in the shelter that Francis had to chalk little boundaries on the ceiling. The brothers would then sleep beneath their own chalk mark, approximately, because some were fat and some skinny, some tall and others short. No one minded then and any of them would have been glad to sleep outside in the snow, so great was their love for the poor Jesus of Nazareth.

...

As more and more brothers came into the fraternity, the simplicity of Rivotorto died and a more rigid structure was born. And when this complexity entered into the idyllic days of the woods and fields, Francis knew he must go to the Pope for his wisdom and guidance on what the brothers should do. It was not that he felt the need for some structure for this new community of men who were forming around him, but Francis did want some kind of official sanction for his way of life in poverty and some ecclesiastical protection for his brothers. There were bands of reformers and fanatics roaming the countryside at the time who were leading the common folk down blind alleys of heretical enthusiasm.

...

Francis understood, as every Christian of his time did, that no matter how clear the voice of God sounded within you, there was no assurance that it was in fact God's voice unless the church gave approval. The Roman Court was the discerner of spirits for every Christian of the thirteenth century. So Francis and a few of the brothers set out from Rivotorto on the long walk to Rome.

—Murray Bodo, *Francis: The Journey and the Dream*

APPLICATION TO DAILY LIFE

• How does following Francis's vision call for changes in your life?

• Pray each day that the way of Francis may affect your whole life, that you may truly be a holy person living in the world.

PRAYER

Thank you, Lord, for the faithful ones
who have followed you in the way of St. Francis
through the centuries.
Open my heart and mind
to discern if the Franciscan way of life
is my call to spiritual life.
Amen.

REFLECTION (3)

To Live the Gospel Life

"After the Lord gave me some brothers, no
one showed me what I had to do, but the Most
High Himself revealed to me that I should live
according to the pattern of the Holy Gospel.
And I had this written down simply and in a few
words and the Lord Pope confirmed it for me."

—St. Francis of Assisi, *The Testament*

It is impossible to capture Francis in an analysis or a summary.
Where grace is, there is mystery. But if, in a human way, we try
to list the elements of the mystery, we would have to place the
Gospel at the head of that list. In his delightful and even thrilling
literalness, Francis simply said, "Here is God's living Word. He is
speaking to us today."

What Francis meant by "Gospel" was Jesus, the living Word
of God made living flesh and living with us today. "Brothers,
I know Holy Writ—I know the poor Christ," he said. The last
thing Francis wanted was to be special or to found a group of
people who would be distinguished or superior. He simply
wanted as many people as possible to be led by the Holy Spirit
to live the Gospel of Jesus Christ, allowing the Lord to transform
their lives. To be Franciscan, then, is to attempt to be Christian,
a disciple. So, Franciscans today try to be Christians with the
particular inspiration and traditions of Francis. Nevertheless, the
fundamental thrust is always the Gospel way of life.

A way of life is a set of values, a spirit that affects our whole life,
an attitude that enters into every thought we think, each emotion

we feel, what we say and each action of our days. Christianity is the way of life God himself has graciously given us. Our tradition says: "Since Christ is the way, the truth, and the life, Secular Franciscans should have the deep conviction that, by Baptism and profession they must become like Christ crucified, and follow his Gospel as their rule of life. As they live their lives in the world, they are imbued with the mind and spirit of Christ."

We can never emphasize enough the fact that *Gospel* means "Good News." This is one of the key ideas in Francis's life. He was thrilled to discover the beauty and simplicity of this idea: The Good News is that God is our Father and our Mother! God loves us! Christ is our Brother. We are the children of God, truly possessing spiritual life. We are brothers and sisters of Christ and of each other. The Spirit of God's love lives in us. Our lives are holy and secure in Christ. Christ and his Gospel were, therefore, the center of the life of Francis. To live like Francis, we are to live the Gospel—that is, live according to the Good News, live as God's children, brothers and sisters of Christ, temples of the Holy Spirit. Practically every detail of life has been modeled for us on the earthly life of Christ.

Franciscan life is a high calling. But if God has given us this vocation, he will also give us his grace to carry it out. One important quality is required: a spirit of trust and generosity. This is the lesson of Francis's life: a spirit of childlike confidence in his Father in heaven, and in the power and wisdom and love of his Father. With him, there is nothing to fear. Nothing can hurt us. There is no problem we cannot solve with God's wisdom and grace.

QUESTIONS FOR REFLECTION

- What does a Franciscan spirituality add to the Christian way of life?

- What is the Good News?
- How are we told how to live the Gospel life?

CONNECTING WITH SCRIPTURE

Now after John was arrested, Jesus came to Galilee, proclaiming the good news of God, and saying, "The time is fulfilled, and the kingdom of God has come near; repent, and believe in the good news."

As Jesus passed along the Sea of Galilee, he saw Simon and his brother Andrew casting a net into the sea—for they were fishermen. And Jesus said to them, "Follow me and I will make you fish for people." And immediately they left their nets and followed him. As he went a little farther, he saw James son of Zebedee and his brother John, who were in their boat mending the nets. Immediately he called them; and they left their father Zebedee in the boat with the hired men, and followed him.

—Mark 1:14–20

CONNECTING WITH FRANCISCAN WRITINGS

Brother Bernard was, in Francis' eyes, the real founder of the Order of Lesser Brothers, because he was the first wealthy Assisian to sell all his possessions, give them to the poor, and throw himself completely upon the mercy of God. Francis remembered so vividly the night he spent in the home of the wealthy merchant, Bernard of Quintavalle. Bernard, pretending to be asleep, had spent the night watching Francis at prayer, and in the morning had told Francis of his resolve to renounce his possessions and to follow Francis in the footsteps of Christ.

Francis was utterly stunned. Never, in his wildest hopes, had he imagined that God would so quickly answer his prayers for companionship in poverty and pursuit of the Dream. But he did not immediately show his joy and relief to Bernard. Instead, Francis said that they must go together to the bishop's house where there was a poor priest who would say Mass for them. Afterward they would ask the priest to open the Book of the Gospels three times to see what God would there reveal to them about their future; whether Bernard was to follow Christ as Francis' brother, or not.

Francis' heart always beat faster when he recalled those three openings of the Gospels:

"If you wish to be perfect, go and sell all your possessions, and give to the poor...and come, follow me."

"Take nothing for your journey, neither staff nor knapsack, shoes nor money."

"Anyone who will come after me must renounce self, take up the cross and follow me."

—Murray Bodo, *Francis: The Journey and the Dream*

APPLICATION TO DAILY LIFE

- Do you think of your life as an observance of the Gospel?
- Why was Francis so concerned about the Gospel life?
- If the Gospel is the Good News, should our lives and our faith be glad or sad?
- Think of practical ways to apply the Gospel to your daily life at home, in the workplace, among friends.

PRAYER

I praise you, Lord, for the Good News,
your Gospel of truth
which can lead me to life's great truth.
Keep me faithful to your teachings.
Amen.

....
Franciscan Spirituality: God Is Love

"Most High, all-powerful, good Lord,
Yours are the praises, the glory, and the honor,
and all blessing,
To You alone, Most High, do they belong,
   and no human is worthy to mention Your
   name.
...
Praise and bless my Lord and give Him thanks
   and serve Him with great humility."
                    —St. Francis of Assisi, *The Testament*

A spirituality is a particular way, or emphasis, in following Christ. Obviously many things are common to all Christians, and these are more important than the interests of any one group of Christians: Christlike love and forgiveness, community, personal and communal prayer, celebration of the sacramental life, obedience to legitimate authority, love of Scripture, and concern for justice and peace, to name a few. There is no difference between our goals and our ways and means. But there can be a difference in emphasis.

Differing spiritualities depend largely on the personalities of their founders and the times in which religious communities developed. We speak of a Benedictine spirituality, inspired by the monastic vision of St. Benedict. A Dominican spirituality will be marked by the teaching and preaching fervor of St. Dominic. Francis's spirituality was simply to "observe the Gospel." Yet, because he was a unique and attractive personality, the Church gained a unique charism called Franciscan spirituality.

There is also a spirituality proper to lay people, as contrasted with that of priests; a lay spirituality is properly more concerned with activities in the world than being about the business of the church and liturgical rituals. This idea featured prominently in the documents of the Second Vatican Council.

Pius XII described Franciscan spirituality this way: "There is, then, a Franciscan doctrine in accordance with which God is holy, is great, and above all, is good, indeed the supreme Good. For in this doctrine, God is love. He lives by love, creates for love, becomes flesh and redeems, that is, he saves and makes holy, for love. There is also a Franciscan way of contemplating Jesus...in his human love."

The great emphasis, then, is on the fact that God is love. Every Christian believes this, of course, but some of us choose to emphasize it as Francis did.

To live the Gospel according to the spirit of Francis means participating
- in communion with Christ poor and crucified,
- in the love of God,
- in brother/sisterhood with all people and all of creation,
- in the life and mission of the Church,
- in continual conversion,
- in a life of prayer—liturgical, personal, communal,
- as instruments of peace.

QUESTIONS FOR REFLECTION

- Why are there differences between various Christian spiritualities?
- What is your image of God?
- What is unique about Franciscan spirituality?
- Why does Francis's way attract you?

CONNECTING WITH SCRIPTURE

Then someone came to him and said, "Teacher, what good deed must I do to have eternal life?" And he said to him, "Why do you ask me about what is good? There is only one who is good. If you wish to enter into life, keep the commandments." He said to him, "Which ones?" And Jesus said, "You shall not murder; You shall not commit adultery; You shall not steal; You shall not bear false witness; Honor your father and mother; also, You shall love your neighbor as yourself." The young man said to him, "I have kept all these; what do I still lack?" Jesus said to him, "If you wish to be perfect, go, sell your possessions, and give the money to the poor, and you will have treasure in heaven; then come, follow me." When the young man heard this word, he went away grieving, for he had many possessions.

—Matthew 19:16–22

CONNECTING WITH FRANCISCAN WRITINGS

Francis had noticed from the beginning that when he went begging, especially, very few people looked into his eyes. They seemed always to avoid eye contact, either from embarrassment or fear or contempt. There were, of course, the few bright-eyed, open people whose eyes were surely the lamps of their whole selves radiating love and goodness and trust.

It was marvelous how people became who they really were once you reached out your hand to them in the gesture of the beggar. Even the insight into people he had gained in his father's shop paled when compared to what he learned begging in the streets of Assisi. So often the veneer of respectability would be sloughed off and something like a monster would emerge, cursing and destroying you with the venom of words and gestures. It was an experience only beggars understood.

From these harrowing experiences Francis determined to be always on the outside what he was on the inside. He knew that some of the brothers felt he overdid this obsession with sincerity and wholeness, but Francis feared duplicity and hypocrisy more than anything in all the world. It was against hypocrisy that Jesus had railed again and again in the Gospels, and Francis was sure Jesus would never speak harshly against anything unless it spoiled the human heart and made the Holy Spirit's entry there impossible.

—Murray Bodo, *Francis: The Journey and the Dream*

APPLICATION TO DAILY LIFE

- What might the quote "God is love" imply for your worries, your prayer, your work, your family life, and your relationships with others?
- Does the fact that you are attracted to the Franciscan way indicate anything special about your personality?
- This week, try to recall, as often as you can, the simple reality that "God is love."

PRAYER

Lord,
I invite your Spirit to guide me
into your way,
into your love.
I will try to follow you
all the days of my life.
Amen.

Christ Is Our Brother in God's Love

We should wish for nothing else and have no
other desire; we should find no pleasure or delight
in anything except in our Creator, Redeemer, and
Savior; he alone is true God, who is perfect good,
all good, every good, the true and supreme good,
and he alone is good, loving and gentle, kind and
understanding; he alone is holy, just, true, and
right; he alone is kind, innocent, pure, and from
him, through him, and in him is all pardon, all
grace, and all glory for the penitent, the just, and
the blessed who rejoice in heaven.

—St. Francis of Assisi, the Rule of 1221

St. Francis never tired of speaking about God's goodness. He
could not think of enough wonderful names to give him.

Above all, Francis thought of God as his good Father. In
Francis's rediscovery of Christ in the Gospel, he found that Christ
continually called upon his Father, doing all things for love of his
Father. Christ makes us his brothers and sisters. He gives us his
own Father, the most loving parent!

God possesses all the goodness, beauty, and happiness that
the human mind can imagine—and infinitely more than we can
envision. God is infinitely, eternally, unimaginably good. God is
infinite love. And God wants us to share that goodness!

Love is a sharing in God's own Spirit. There is something
mysterious about it because it is divine. Love manifests itself in a
myriad of ways which we notice when we are observant. God is

not bound by limitations. God's love is an infinite torrent wider than the universe, flowing within the community called Father, Son and Spirit, and then pouring out on the whole world. Jesus is the sign of this love, captured and emptied out into a body and spirit like ours. His love was divine—he gave us all he had, even his life. Yet his love was also human—even Jesus had to make judgments about what to give, when to give, what not to do, what was wise now, what tomorrow. He had to consider what others' needs really were and the best way to fill them.

Love simply must expand, radiating its light and warmth in all directions. The happier we are, the more we want to tell others, to share our happiness with them. God, who is Love itself, also wanted to share goodness with others. God was not forced to share this goodness; God wanted to! God wanted to be our Father, to give us divine life, goodness, and happiness.

The greatest thing God could give us was life—not only human life but a sharing in his own life. This mystery is called grace. Grace affects us at the very roots of our being. We are as new as the day we were first created. Yet the newness is not something added on top of what we already are. It soaks our nature, permeates our being—if we let it. This means that the very power whereby God loves is our power. The very wisdom and intelligence with which God loves is ours. The very giving and going out, the generosity and feeling is all ours, for what is in God is in us, not by some kind of distant imitation but by our participation in God's own life.

Jesus showed us this life of grace that is God's love. He won for us our new creation through his own Spirit so that we might live the life of God in human form, as Jesus did. God did not give us Jesus "outside" of ourselves only—a man who lived two thousand years ago—or even the Risen Christ up there on the altar. God gives us himself, Jesus, his Spirit inside us as fire is inside wood without being the same as the wood.

If we let it, and in accord with our human limitations, we experience this new creation of our very being. No transforming power surpasses the power of love. A man or woman in love is a new person. So are we if we let God's gracious gift of his own life soak into us.

We have said that the first emphasis of Franciscan spirituality is the realization that God is love. The second is that Christ is our brother in God's love, and we are all brothers and sisters in Christ. Francis rediscovered the plain truth of the Gospels: Christ is not only God; he is human. He is a true man with a real body, real mind, real will, real emotions, just like all his brothers and sisters, minus sin and the personal results of sin. Jesus, our brother, came that we might have life forever with God our Father.

The Gospel life is simply to love as Jesus loved, as a human, knowing that it is God's love pulsing within us. The Gospel life is to love people—not people in general, but these people, the ones we meet, the ones we live with or work with, the ones who may cause us difficulty or pain, as well as the ones who bring us joy.

We never forget the central theme: Behind it all, in it all, and through it all is the God who is love. Our response within all the everyday responses of daily life is, "Blessed be God because he is good."

QUESTIONS FOR REFLECTION

- What does it mean to love another? Do you see that there is mystery as well as everydayness about it?
- What is God's greatest gift to us?

CONNECTING WITH SCRIPTURE

As the Father has loved me, so I have loved you; abide in my love. If you keep my commandments, you will abide in my love, just as I have kept my Father's commandments and abide in his love. I have said these things to you so that my joy may be in you, and that your joy may be complete.

This is my commandment, that you love one another as I have loved you. No one has greater love than this, to lay down one's life for one's friends. You are my friends if you do what I command you. I do not call you servants any longer, because the servant does not know what the master is doing; but I have called you friends, because I have made known to you everything that I have heard from my Father. You did not choose me but I chose you. And I appointed you to go and bear fruit, fruit that will last, so that the Father will give you whatever you ask him in my name. I am giving you these commands so that you may love one another.

—John 15:9–17

CONNECTING WITH FRANCISCAN WRITINGS

To Francis everything in him and around him was a gift from his Father in Heaven. He expected nothing, so he was grateful for everything. Even a piece of earth was cause for rejoicing, and he thanked God always for everything that was. He held everything to his heart with the enthusiasm of a child surprised by some unexpected toy. The air he breathed, the sounds he heard, the sights and smells of all the world entered his grateful soul through senses perfected by gratitude and purity of heart. Nothing was evil, for everything came from God, and evil came only from a heart that chose not to love. The heart through passion or selfishness or pride could choose not to love and that was evil, but no thing or no person was evil in and of itself.

...

And he was not worried or anxious about yesterday, today, or tomorrow because Christ is, and all things are in Him and He is in the Father. Francis no longer worried, not because he was a naive optimist, but because he had become in prayer and penance a realist who saw the unimportance of everything but God, and in God and with God and through God, the importance of everything. God was everywhere; the divine presence charged creation with a power and glory that made everything shine with beauty and goodness in Francis' eyes. God's touch on everything inspirited everything that was.

Francis wanted more than anything else to leave behind in everyone an attitude of celebration. Union with God, with every man, with every woman, with every child, with every thing was love, and love brought joy, not gloom. When religion was gloom, then the heart had gone out of it and Christ's warning against pharisaical observance had been forgotten.

—Murray Bodo, *Francis: The Journey and the Dream*

APPLICATION TO DAILY LIFE

- What is your idea of love? Can you name the people who gave you your idea of love?
- What can God's parental love mean in your life? What is the greatest quality of a loving parent?
- Have you ever thought of Christ as your brother? How can you love him more?
- Try to realize and repeat often: "God is love. God is my loving parent. Christ is my brother. I want to love them and give them goodness in return."

PRAYER

You are love, charity.
You are wisdom; You are humility; You are patience
(cf. Psalm 70:5);
You are beauty; You are meekness; You are security;
You are inner peace; You are joy; You are our hope and joy;

You are justice; You are moderation; You are all our riches;
(You are enough for us).
You are beauty; You are meekness;
You are the protector
(cf. Psalm 30:5).
You are our guardian and defender;
You are strength; You are refreshment
(cf. Psalm 42:2).
You are our hope; You are our faith; You are our charity;
You are all our sweetness;
You are our eternal life:
Great and wonderful Lord,
God almighty, Merciful Savior.

—St. Francis, The Praises of God

....
Christ, the Masterpiece, Planned from Eternity

"He is the image of the invisible God, the
firstborn of all creation; for in him all things were
created.... He himself is before all things."

—Colossians 1:15–17

Imagine the eternal God being able to express all his love
in a single gift: infinite, eternal, unspeakable life and love
concentrated in an individual being. That gift is Jesus.

God has an eternal plan to share himself with intelligent, free,
loving beings whom he would create not just as beings who are
somewhat like him, because they can think and love and act, but
who love with the power of his love, judge with his wisdom, love
not just with human life but with a sharing of divine life itself,
which possesses their being.

God's plan is centered in Jesus. Jesus is the eternal model of
all God's children. Through Jesus, divine life was given to all his
brothers and sisters. He is the source through whom divine life
lives in a human body and flows to every human being on earth.
All things were made in him, through him, and for him. He is the
first adorer, the perfect child, the model creature, the "firstborn of
all creation," and the firstborn of many brothers and sisters.

God the eternal Son, at one point in time, became God made
human. But every creature before and after him, the first to the
last man and woman on earth, was made in his image, destined to
be saved by him, drawn to God through him. He is "the meeting
place of uncreated and created love."

Christ is the image of God, but God had in mind countless images of Christ. Mary, the mother to be, was the first of these. Then came all the other brothers and sisters of Christ, every human being on earth. Whether a man or a woman knows Christ or will ever hear of Christ, he or she is saved by Christ, loved by Christ, called to Christ. If our first parents are with God, it is because they were saved by the death and Resurrection of Christ.

Only one real calamity occurred in all human history. That is sin, cutting us off from God's plan. Humanity threw away its relationship with God and turned to being self-sufficient, self-centered, attempting to find redemption apart from God's plan.

The redeeming grace of Christ is offered to every human being because everyone belongs to Christ. Each is called to be healed and raised up to share the life and victory of Jesus, the first man. The masterpiece, the head and source of creation, is its redeemer. The model for all is the model for those who must suffer the blight of sin on their lives. Jesus emptied himself, entering into our life as it has been damaged by sin. Without sin himself and without the moral effects of sin, he nevertheless experienced the sinful condition of the world. Ultimately this power of evil killed him, but because he forgave sin and trusted his Father, Jesus rose to a new and eternal life. He can now give that life to us with a power that cannot be stopped. His Spirit lives in us. Therefore, we are able to conquer sin and death with his power.

By the seeming failure of his death, Jesus becomes the irresistible destroyer of sin and the giver of life. He has power: gentle but infinite, divine but humanly channeled. He is king. His law is the Spirit within us. His kingdom is grace. His punishment is forgiveness. His power is humility. His treasure is love. St. Francis was thrilled with this great and simple idea of Christ at the center of creation, not only as God but as the man who became the world's victim, priest, and king. The great victory of the Resurrection meant that evil is destroyed forever, and death has lost its sting.

Francis saw himself as the "Herald of the Great King." A herald is one who comes with a royal message. Francis came singing the Good News from the King of Kings: God is love; Christ is our brother who gives us life, saves us, and brings us to the Kingdom of the Good God. Every action we perform, therefore, must somehow be an act of loyal love.

QUESTIONS FOR REFLECTION

- Why did God will the creation of the world?
- Who is God's eternal masterpiece? Why? Who are images of the masterpiece?
- Why did Francis call himself the "Herald of the Great King"?

CONNECTING WITH SCRIPTURE

He is the image of the invisible God, the firstborn of all creation; for in him all things in heaven and on earth were created, things visible and invisible, whether thrones or dominions or rulers or powers—all things have been created through him and for him. He himself is before all things, and in him all things hold together. He is the head of the body, the church; he is the beginning, the firstborn from the dead, so that he might come to have first place in everything. For in him all the fullness of God was pleased to dwell, and through him God was pleased to reconcile to himself all things, whether on earth or in heaven, by making peace through the blood of his cross.

—Colossians 1:15–20

CONNECTING WITH FRANCISCAN WRITINGS

Francis loved to sing. It freed his spirit and turned the human voice, so often an organ of selfishness and sin, into an instrument of celebration.... He was simply giving voice to the joy within him and to the beauty he saw all around him. Whenever he felt his heart constricting again, he would break into a song of joy and praise.... Francis loved that image of himself as a lute strung for rapture. He wanted to stand in the wind of April afternoons and let the Holy Spirit play upon him for all the world to hear the beauty of his music. And in every season he tried to be strung and tuned for the hand of Jesus to play upon His poor little instrument, made perfect and resonant by the skill of Jesus Himself.

—Murray Bodo, *Francis: The Journey and the Dream*

APPLICATION TO DAILY LIFE

- Devotion to the king means loyalty, generosity, and courage in the daily business of living and thinking and loving. How will you show devotion today?
- Every moment of life should have reference to Christ. Consider this often. For example, how are you involved in helping to heal or redeem the world in your life?
- Pray each day: "Blessed is He who comes as King, in the name of the Lord! Peace in heaven, and glory in the highest!"

PRAYER

We adore you, Lord Jesus Christ,
here and in all your churches in the whole world,
and we bless you,
because by your holy cross, you have redeemed the world.
Amen

REFLECTION (7)

The Grace of Christ

"I came that they might have life, and have it abundantly."

—John 10:10

race means "free," gratis. In a sense, we can say that everything God gives us is freely given, for we certainly can't earn it. But the special freedom of grace is that it's so special we wouldn't even have thought of it. The unexpected gift is the grace to live on God's level: not to be God but to have God's life—not just glorious, intelligent, free human life, but God's kind of decision-making, God's unconditional loving and God's way of living.

For all our glorious human gifts, we could not look upon the face of God, speak to God directly, think God's thoughts, love with love as perfect as God's, through our own power. This is the divine gift that our Father has given us in Jesus. To our nature—all that would be expected to belong to a normal human being—God joins his own life. This is the most gracious act possible—the freest of all free gifts.

Actually, there never was a natural man or woman. From eternity God planned to make us his real children with his own life in us, not just a natural life. Maybe it's because we've had this special calling that we sometimes think we have a right to it—as if it were part of our nature.

So much for the necessary distinctions. When we try to realize what this gracious gift is, we had best take the words of Jesus: "Because I live, you also will live. On that day you will know that

29

I am in my Father, and you in me, and I in you. They who have my commandments and keep them are those who love me; and those who love me will be loved by my Father.... Those who love me will keep my word, and my Father will love them; and we will come to them and make our home with them" (John 14:19).

Grace is what the Bible is about—all that God eternally wanted to give us, the reason Christ became man, the purpose of his sending his Spirit within us. God raises us up to him, and we are his friends.

Grace, then, refers to the relationship of love between God and his children. We are changed to the roots of our being when God recreates us. It's as if God made a statue out of nothing and then recreated the statue into a beautiful human being. Our life is graced. It has a divine quality put there by God.

God always wants to deepen and enrich grace in us. He is constantly calling us to be open to his presence so that we can more and more be possessed with the vision he has of the world, with the boundless love with which he cares for all his creatures, with the power that no other power can withstand.

"Everything is grace!" St. Paul said. We must constantly try to understand our relationship with God as the very heart of our life.

QUESTIONS FOR REFLECTION
- What does *grace* mean literally?
- How would you describe grace?

CONNECTING WITH SCRIPTURE
Blessed be the God and Father of our Lord Jesus Christ, who has blessed us in Christ with every spiritual blessing in the heavenly places, just as he chose us in Christ before the foundation of the world to be holy and blameless before him in love. He destined us for adoption as his children through Jesus Christ, according to

the good pleasure of his will, to the praise of his glorious grace that he freely bestowed on us in the Beloved. In him we have redemption through his blood, the forgiveness of our trespasses, according to the riches of his grace that he lavished on us. With all wisdom and insight he has made known to us the mystery of his will, according to his good pleasure that he set forth in Christ, as a plan for the fullness of time, to gather up all things in him, things in heaven and things on earth. In Christ we have also obtained an inheritance, having been destined according to the purpose of him who accomplishes all things according to his counsel and will, so that we, who were the first to set our hope on Christ, might live for the praise of his glory. In him you also, when you had heard the word of truth, the gospel of your salvation, and had believed in him, were marked with the seal of the promised Holy Spirit; this is the pledge of our inheritance toward redemption as God's own people, to the praise of his glory.

—Ephesians 1:3–14

CONNECTING WITH FRANCISCAN WRITINGS

One day, when [Francis] was wondering over the mercy of the Lord with regard to the gifts bestowed upon him, he wished that the course of his own life and that of his brothers might be shown him by the Lord; he sought out a place of prayer, as he had done so often, and he persevered there for a long time with fear and trembling, standing before the Lord of the whole earth, and he thought in the bitterness of his soul of the years he had spent wretchedly, frequently repeating this word: "O God, be merciful to me the sinner." Little by little a certain unspeakable joy and very great sweetness began to flood his innermost heart. He began also to stand aloof from himself, and, as his feelings were checked and the darkness that had gathered in his heart because of his fear of sin dispelled, there was poured into him a certainty that all his sins had been forgiven and a confidence of his restoration to grace was given him. He was then caught up above himself, and absorbed in a certain light; the capacity of his mind was enlarged and he could see clearly what was to come to pass. When this sweetness finally passed, along with the light, renewed in spirit, he seemed changed into another man.

—Thomas of Celano, *The Life of St. Francis*

APPLICATION TO DAILY LIFE

- Life is movement. We move with Christ's power. Try to be conscious of God's sanctifying power in your life.
- Our lives are all about growing into God's life. Thank God for this gift, today.

PRAYER

O God, it overwhelms me
to think that you live in me.
What an awesome God you are
to come to one like me.
Enable me to yield my will to your grace
each moment of my life.
Amen.

REFLECTION (8)

Jesus Is Visible Today

> "It is of the essence of the Church that she be both human and divine, visible and yet invisibly endowed, eager to act and yet devoted to contemplation, present in this world and yet not at home in it."
>
> —Constitution on the Sacred Liturgy, 2

Jesus is the Word made flesh. He is God made visible. He is God showing himself in human terms. God adapted himself to our way of communicating—that is, by sight, hearing, touch, taste, and smell. Jesus was something people could "handle" as St. John says. They could see him, hear him, touch him. If Jesus spoke to you, God spoke. If he forgave you, God forgave you.

God's communication of himself was to go on after Jesus's death. The risen Jesus is no longer visible, audible, touchable, but he left another sacrament like himself. Not just one body, but a body formed by many bodies, many persons—the followers of Christ. Until the end of time, the Church is the sign or sacrament or visibility of Christ. The Church bears the burden and the glory of saying to the world, "If you want to see and hear the love and forgiveness of Jesus, look at us, listen to us."

Through this weak and wonderful, glorious and humiliated body, Jesus acts today. "Not many of you were wise or noble when you were first called," said Paul to his Corinthian community. Yet that is what God chooses to use as his continuing self-communication, the ongoing redemptive work of Jesus until the end of time.

People always seem to itch to have some kind of superchurch: pure, entirely spiritual, untouched by structure, organization, human weakness, limitation, and sin. But such an unreal dream forgets our human nature. We are embodied people. We are human only if we are whole: spirit expressing itself bodily.

God not only emptied himself in becoming human. He continues the hiding of his divine glory beneath the unlikely form of a body of people called Christians, united by his Spirit and diverse as their many temperaments, cultures, and histories.

Many reformers existed in St. Francis's day, and every one of them had a real complaint. Many of the clergy were not worthy of the name. Wealth was a bigger factor in Church life than Jesus ever would have wished. The Church really needed a reform in its clergy, if not in its head, the pope. Most of these reforms were shipwrecked on the rocks of their own rebelliousness. They tried to impose a reform on the Church from without. They would cure the Church if they had to kill it in the process. But Francis—who could spot a greedy priest or hypocritical bishop as well as anyone—preserved a pure and simple reverence for priests and a loyal obedience to the pope that many today would call "unenlightened." If God were going to do any good for his Church through Francis, Francis believed God would do it within the structure of the Church.

Francis saw the mystery of the Church: new wine in new wineskins, divine life pulsing through arteries sometimes clogged with spiritual cholesterol, her healing of the world hampered because her hands had become weak or arthritic. But this is the Church that exists: a body of people united in Jesus, breathing his love into the world, perpetuating his death and Resurrection—but in the glorious and inglorious ups and downs of everyday human life.

The faults of the Church are evident. What we need is a constant reminder of the divine glory within it. To be Franciscan is to follow Francis in trying to lead the Gospel life where Francis lived it: within the Church, that inefficient and ridiculous pilgrim walking the way of the cross, yet already alive with the life of the risen Christ.

QUESTIONS FOR REFLECTION

- How is tension between the spirit of the Church and its visible structure a healthy one?
- How would you describe Francis's relationship to problems in the Church?

CONNECTING WITH SCRIPTURE

For just as the body is one and has many members, and all the members of the body, though many, are one body, so it is with Christ. For in the one Spirit we were all baptized into one body— Jews or Greeks, slaves or free—and we were all made to drink of one Spirit.

... God arranged the members in the body, each one of them, as he chose. If all were a single member, where would the body be? As it is, there are many members, yet one body. The eye cannot say to the hand, "I have no need of you," nor again the head to the feet, "I have no need of you." ... If one member suffers, all suffer together with it; if one member is honored, all rejoice together with it.

Now you are the body of Christ and individually members of it.
—see 1 Corinthians 12:12–31

CONNECTING WITH FRANCISCAN WRITINGS

It is one of the wonders of life that we meet souls compatible with our own in places and circumstances unexpected and surprising. This fact never so thoroughly overwhelmed Francis as in his audience with Pope Innocent III. This magnificent man had Francis' own suspicions and mistrust of anything that smacked of fanaticism, and in Francis' first meeting with the Pope, he had sensed the Pope's mind working intensely behind the fixed and penetrating gaze. His eyes were like shafts of light illuminating the dark corners of Francis' soul. And when the audience was over, Francis had no idea what the Pope really felt. Everything was in abeyance.

That night, as Innocent later related to Francis, the Pope dreamed that the Church of St. John Lateran, the mother church of Christendom, began to lean on its side and topple to the ground. Then, just as the nightmare was pounding most loudly in the Pope's brain and the church was crashing to the ground, a little beggar leaped from the shadows and supported the falling building on his own shoulders. The Pope, waking with a shudder of relief, recognized the beggar as Francis, the poor man from Assisi.

Now Innocent never put much stock in nightmares, but there was about this dream the power and persuasion of a vision, and he resummoned Francis and the brothers the following day. It was at this audience that Francis saw in Pope Innocent a heart like his own. The Pope's whole personality radiated the intensity and seriousness of a child. And unlike most other people to whom Francis had stretched out his hands in supplication, this man looked straight into his eyes. Francis would never forget their complete candor and innocence.

—Murray Bodo, *Francis: The Journey and the Dream*

APPLICATION TO DAILY LIFE

- How do you believe you are important as a member of the body of Christ?
- What can you do to make the Church more convincing and attractive?
- What temptations to a purely spiritual Church do you have?

- Think of three specific things to do on a regular basis to benefit the body of Christ.

PRAYER

Lord Jesus, as a member of the body of Christ,
I can be your hand to help another,
your voice to sing praise,
your heart to love the Church into wholeness.
Praise you, Jesus, for making me a part of your body.
Please show me how to use this precious gift
to help "thy Kingdom come."
Amen.

The Real Christ

"O Lord Jesus Christ, I entreat you to give me
two graces before I die: First, that in my lifetime
I may feel in body and soul as far as possible the
pain You endured, dear Lord, in the hour of Your
most bitter suffering; and second, that I may feel
in my heart as far as possible that excess of love
by which You, O Son of God, were inflamed to
undertake so cruel a suffering for us sinners."

—*The Little Flowers of St. Francis*

In front of the altar of the friary chapel of Greccio, Italy, you
can still see the large stone, with a V-like hollow on top, which
St. Francis used as his Christmas crib, thereby popularizing a
devotion we still have today.

The crib and the cross were the two loves of Jesus's life—the
mystery of the Incarnation of the eternal God and the mystery of
his giving up that life.

Christians are often so busy proving that Jesus is God that they
sometimes de-emphasize the fact that he is truly human, with all
the feelings and experiences, joys and sorrows of our human life.
When we say that he had no sin or any personal result of sin,
we somehow feel that he was exempt from emotion, temptation,
limitation, problems.

The baby in the crib of Bethlehem is a statement of the goodness
of human life. It was as if God said, "Do you doubt the goodness
of what I have created? I will enter into it as it is. Not only as it is
damaged by sin, but as it is human."

The baby Francis saw in the crib would grow like any other baby, since Christ would not have been a true human being if he had never been faced with the need of depending on others for care, of making up his mind, of choosing freely, or of taking one course rather than another—at a time when both looked good. When he prayed, his knees felt the hard ground beneath his bones like anyone else's. When he drank wine, it exhilarated his body and spirit like anyone else's. He knew the courage and discipline required to get up and go to work every day. When frustration or failure fell on his path, he had to exercise patience like anyone else. People ignored him, misjudged him, slandered him, and finally killed him. It cost him the same effort of courage, trust in his Father, forgiveness that these things cost us every day.

He sensed who he was, but this knowledge need not have been sharp and clear. He was appointed Messiah from eternity, but the Jewish boy and young man had to learn, by prayer and openness, that the real path of the Messiah was in the suffering servant of Isaiah. When he faced death, he cried out in terror just as we do. And when he put his life into the hands of his Father, the gift was made in the dark. Certainly his Father had said he would raise him up: He says the same to us. But the passing to the Father was nevertheless an act of trust made in the darkness.

The actual physical sufferings of Christ were a constant object of Francis's meditation. The literal-minded poet saw the hard facts: It's what you put on the line that shows how dedicated you are. Jesus held nothing back. He deliberately walked into Jerusalem knowing what would happen to him. Jesus wanted to swallow, as it were, all the misery that sin had brought into the world. He let it fill him, possess him in the same way that he wanted to possess others by love. He let it ruin all his plans, scare away his friends, and finally destroy him.

But sinful men had not counted on one thing: being forgiven. Jesus destroyed the power of sinful men by forgiving them. When they did their worst, he did his best. At the heart of salvation are three words, "Father, forgive them."

Contemplating the birth of Jesus and his crucifixion brought Francis to the boundaries of joy and sadness. Francis would be so exhilarated at the beauty of the Incarnation that he would take two sticks and act as if he were playing the violin, praising God in song. Pondering the painful suffering of Jesus's crucifixion would cause Francis to cry agonizing tears of compassion for his suffering Savior.

We follow Francis in the divine ups and downs of life. Every day is up—letting the vision of faith see the beauty of God's love saving the world, letting him reveal the world of the human Christ. Every day is down—giving up a selfish use of that world by dying to selfishness in all its disguises: dying to revenge and greediness, cruelty and lust, laziness and bossiness. Thereby we live through another up—another rising with Christ to richer, deeper, more joyful companionship with him. Death and resurrection every day is as prosaic as Nazareth, painful as Calvary, glorious as Easter morning.

QUESTIONS FOR REFLECTION

• What particular activities in your life can you see Jesus experiencing if he walked the earth today?
• What might it mean to die daily?
• What might it mean to resurrect daily?

CONNECTING WITH SCRIPTURE

In those days a decree went out from Emperor Augustus that all the world should be registered. This was the first registration and was taken while Quirinius was governor of Syria. All went to their own towns to be registered. Joseph also went from the town of Nazareth in Galilee to Judea, to the city of David called Bethlehem, because he was descended from the house and family of David. He went to be registered with Mary, to whom he was engaged and who was expecting a child. While they were there, the time came for her to deliver her child. And she gave birth to her firstborn son and wrapped him in bands of cloth, and laid him in a manger, because there was no place for them in the inn.

In that region there were shepherds living in the fields, keeping watch over their flock by night. Then an angel of the Lord stood before them, and the glory of the Lord shone around them, and they were terrified. But the angel said to them, "Do not be afraid; for see—I am bringing you good news of great joy for all the people: to you is born this day in the city of David a Savior, who is the Messiah, the Lord. This will be a sign for you: you will find a child wrapped in bands of cloth and lying in a manger."

—see Luke 2:1–20

CONNECTING WITH FRANCISCAN WRITINGS

Someone to love, someone to care for. It was that thought which gripped his heart at Greccio that Christmas he had decided to celebrate the Birth of Jesus in a new way. He had brought a real ox and ass to the altar so that they, too, could share in this rebirth of Christ in the bread and wine of the Christmas Eucharist. At Christmas it was the infant Christ who was born again in human hearts, and it struck Francis that God came to earth as a baby so that we would have someone to care for. Christmas was the dearest of feasts because it meant that God was now one of us. Flesh of our flesh and bone of our bone, this child we could approach without fear.

...

Someone to love. That was Greccio; that was Christmas. He prayed for all the lonely people of the world that they would understand what God's enfleshment meant to them personally. God was like us now in everything but sin. And He let Himself be touched and handled by everyone who would come to Him. Someone to care for, someone to touch. That was Greccio; that was God become a man.

—Murray Bodo, *Francis: The Journey and the Dream*

APPLICATION TO DAILY LIFE

• Think of yourself as one who shares in the holiness of God. How does this view of yourself affect your choices and daily activity?

• Choose three actions this week to do deliberately and joyfully in union with Christ. Visualize yourself walking and talking with Jesus as you carry out these actions.

PRAYER

Help me, Lord, to seek you in all the events of my life,
to praise you in good times and in troubled moments.
Enable me to bear the crosses of my life as you bore yours—
with courage and with faith.
Amen.

The Gift of the Spirit

"Then he entered into the city of Assisi and
began, as though drunk with the Holy Spirit, to
praise God aloud in the streets and the squares."
—*Legend of the Three Companions*

The earliest biography thus describes Francis's actions after he
had stripped himself of everything in the world—even his
clothing, which he had laid at the feet of his angry and bewildered
father. Now he was free, and the Spirit within him found no
obstacle to complete possession.

Another early biographer describes Francis's reaction when at
Mass he heard the words of Christ about having neither gold nor
silver, scrip nor bread, neither shoes nor two garments. Francis, he
says, was "seized" by the Holy Spirit and joyfully cried out, "This
is what I want; this is what I seek; this I will do with all my heart!"

The Holy Spirit is not an extra in Christian holiness. Rather,
the sending of the Spirit is the completing of the entire beautiful
plan of God to share his Life with us. Jesus "emptied himself"
and took our human nature. As our brother, he let himself be
possessed fully by the Spirit. The Spirit powered him through
a human life like ours, led him into a loving sacrificial death.
Because Jesus emptied himself totally in trust and love, he could
be raised in victory to the eternal glory he had with the Father
and the Spirit. But now—and only now, after his death—could the
victorious God-man Savior send his Spirit, the Spirit of the Father,
to complete his work on earth.

The Spirit thus takes the place of the absent Jesus. We know very well that Jesus is not really absent. The word refers to the fact that his visible and mortal life is over. All that he came to do can now be made available to all people through his Spirit. The Spirit flows out upon the whole world, as it were, through the pierced heart of Christ.

Only because he suffered could Jesus release the Spirit in this way. "If I do not go away, the Advocate will not come to you" (John 16:7). "No one can enter the kingdom of God without being born of water and the Spirit" (John 3:5).

The Catholic Rite of Confirmation has these words at the actual conferring of the sacrament: "Receive the seal of the Holy Spirit, the Gift of the Father." We can never emphasize enough that the Spirit is the gift God wanted to give from eternity. All that is said about grace, about God's love, about God's eternal plan is summed up in the Spirit—God's gift—himself. There is but one revelation, or self-communication, of God. It comes from the Father through the Son and is completed by the Spirit to the glory of the Father and the Son.

These are unfathomable mysteries. We cannot hope to have this mysterious action of God neatly blueprinted in human sentences. But neither should we restrain our minds and hearts from experiencing as much as possible the infinitely tender coming of God by his Spirit. God is love, and the Spirit is God's love as a gift to us.

The Spirit makes us alive, fully alive as God intended us to be. By opening ourselves to God's offer of himself—our ability to respond is itself his gift—our being is gradually transformed. God's way of loving becomes our way of loving if we allow the Spirit to possess us. God's way of seeing is the way of our own mind unless we let selfishness darken it. We move into deeper understanding of God's ways, greater experience of his loving presence and power in our lives, because "God's love has been poured into our hearts through the Holy Spirit that has been given to us" (Romans 5:5).

Only as people possessed by the Spirit can we rightly estimate the individual gifts of the Spirit. We are made to give glory to God as his children gathered together. Every gift of the Spirit is given for this purpose—our ability to pray, to love and to forgive, to work and to wait, to suffer patiently and to fight valiantly, to walk in the valley of darkness or skip along the mountaintops.

The movement toward Gospel poverty in the Middle Ages was an example of a special charism or gift of the Spirit for the ever-needed renewal of the Church. Francis was gifted with a special charism to be a prominent part of the renewal of the Church of his day. We now open ourselves to all the Spirit wishes to do for the Church today through the continuing spirit of Francis. We are called to be a community of brothers and sisters under one Father, bound together for the sake of Christ and through his love, brothers and sisters in the Spirit.

QUESTIONS FOR REFLECTION

- What phrase or word best expresses your experience of the Holy Spirit?
- What should the Spirit produce in your life?
- How do you recognize the gifts of the Spirit in your life?

CONNECTING WITH SCRIPTURE

When the day of Pentecost had come, they were all together in one place. And suddenly from heaven there came a sound like the rush of a violent wind, and it filled the entire house where they were sitting. Divided tongues, as of fire, appeared among them, and a tongue rested on each of them. All of them were filled with the Holy Spirit and began to speak in other languages, as the Spirit gave them ability.

...Peter, standing with the eleven, raised his voice and addressed them: "...Listen to what I have to say: Jesus of Nazareth, a man attested to you by God with deeds of power, wonders, and signs that God did through him among you, as you yourselves know— this man, handed over to you according to the definite plan and foreknowledge of God, you crucified and killed by the hands of those outside the law. But God raised him up, having freed him from death, because it was impossible for him to be held in its power."

—see Acts 2:1–24

CONNECTING WITH FRANCISCAN WRITINGS

The Holy Spirit helps us to go beyond our own immediate impressions when we sense that as human beings we are helpless. How can I take my next breath except that God is sustaining me? He did not just create us some years ago, and he didn't just make us part of the creation that came to be billions of years ago. God is always creating, always keeping in existence. And so our very ability to live is a constant gift. All the more then, to be aware that if there is anything good that we do, it's not anything that we ourselves do but rather what God does in us. We also recognize that we do some wrong things, and we know that we can overcome the wrong and do good only because we have God's help. That's where I see the other quotation coming in: "No one can say Jesus is Lord except in the Holy Spirit."

To say that Jesus is Lord means that this person we know as Jesus suffered and died on the cross and then rose again and is in glory with God. But how is that real to us? How can we really believe that? Again it seems like we can say the words easily enough. But can we really mean them and live them out except by having the gift of the Holy Spirit? With the Spirit's help, we can dedicate ourselves to the will of God as Jesus did. When I believe that of myself, I can believe that of others and be led by Francis to see that everyone's life, every good that anybody does is the gift of God's Spirit. Therefore, all the good I see around me is God acting. And not only should I follow Francis and not envy that good, but I can go beyond all of that and see that everyone's good is a manifestation of the action of the Holy Spirit. The holy working of the Holy Spirit that Francis talks about being in each one of us is then permeating all human beings in some way. So should I not be led to appreciate that, not only the good that is done in myself, but the good all around me is God's gift to me?

—Hilarion Kistner, *The Gospels According to Saint Francis*

APPLICATION TO DAILY LIFE

- What is the biggest obstacle in your life to being open to the Spirit?
- What needs of others is the Spirit calling you to recognize and fulfill?
- Try to pay deliberate attention to the Spirit in one prayer, one conversation, one piece of work this week.

PRAYER

Spirit of the living God, I am yours.
Fill me with your wondrous gifts
of love and kindness and wisdom.
Use me to witness to your presence
in my little corner of the world.
Amen.

REFLECTION (11)

Mary, Our Mother and Model

Holy Virgin Mary, there is none like unto you
born in the world among women, daughter and
handmaid of the most high King, the heavenly
Father! Mother of our most holy Lord Jesus
Christ, spouse of the Holy Spirit, pray for us with
Saint Michael the Archangel and all the virtues
of heaven and all the saints, to your most holy,
beloved Son, our Lord and Master. Amen.

—St. Francis of Assisi,
Prayer Before the Holy Office

A s we have seen, the human nature of Christ was God's eternal
masterpiece. Next in his beautiful plan was Mary. She would
receive fullness of grace through Christ. Christ was the new Adam;
he alone could save the human race. It was Adam who lost our
inheritance of grace. But just as the first Adam had an Eve at his
side, so the New Adam, Christ, has at his side a new Eve, Mary.
She could not save us, but Christ allowed her to cooperate in his
saving work.

Mary gave birth to Christ at Bethlehem. But as soon as Christ
began to live on earth, his body began to live, too—the vine
and the branches. Mary gladly said "yes" to Christ's coming—
therefore to the coming of the mystical body. She is the mother of
all who would have life in Christ.

Christ gave her to us as mother. She deliberately and gladly
consented to the litany of sorrows that was needed to open our
Father's house for us. When she spoke her bridal consent to
God, she said, "Be it done to me according to thy word." At that

moment she also consented to become mother to all the children of God in that mysterious, eternal kingdom of which the angel spoke. Mary as mother is the most understandable image of what God's love is for us. If every mother loves her child, how warmly must the perfect mother love her child and her children! And this love can only be a reflection of the infinite love of the Father for his children.

The cradle of the Franciscan Order was the Portiuncula ("The Little Portion"), the poor little chapel outside Assisi that was dedicated to Our Lady of the Angels. It was no accident that this greatest of mothers should stand again at a poor cradle. To Francis, Portiuncula was a royal castle, like that other one at Bethlehem, for poverty was the badge of the noble children of God. He said, "Poverty is a royal virtue, because it shone so brightly in the King and Queen."

A deep and abiding love for Mary, the mother of Christ and our spiritual mother, is a characteristic mark of Franciscan spirituality. Francis's devotion centered around one fact: Mary gave us our brother, Christ, and shared his poverty. She was always to be a special advocate and protector of the Order.

Like all good mothers, Mary teaches us. Above all, she teaches us humility. The sister of poverty in the mind of Francis, humility is nowhere more beautifully expressed than in the song of Mary, the Magnificat. Mary was humble in recognizing her complete unworthiness before God. She trusted confidently in the perfect love of God.

One way to honor Mary is by saying the Crown of the Seven Joys of Mary (known as the Franciscan rosary). Francis's great emphasis on joy is reflected in this devotion begun by one of his followers. We are all in a "vale of tears." We need to share Mary's joy. Perhaps the following thoughts on the Seven Joys will help you as you say this rosary:

(1) The Annunciation. Mary's joy springs from her deep humility. "He looked down kindly on the lowliness of His handmaid." "Be it done to me according to thy word."

(2) The Visitation. The joy of Mary's charity blooms as she hastens to help Elizabeth. No sooner does she possess Christ than she begins to share him with others.

(3) The Birth of Our Lord. Mary's joy in the Divine riches from heaven is now possessed by poor human beings on earth. The joy of poverty lies in seeing where true riches lie.

(4) The Adoration of the Magi. The joy of Mary extends to the Gentiles also (we ourselves!) who will be the newly adopted children of God.

(5) The Finding in the Temple. Mary experiences the joy of finding Christ again, she in innocence and we in penance, all of us in prayer and charity.

(6) Appearance of Christ to Mary after the Resurrection. The joy of Mary's faith blooms when her strong faith on Calvary is rewarded.

(7) The Assumption and Coronation. The joy of her hope is fulfilled even beyond her expectations. "The eye has not seen, nor the ear heard."

QUESTIONS FOR REFLECTION

• How is Mary your mother?
• What virtue does Mary especially teach us?

CONNECTING WITH SCRIPTURE

In those days Mary set out and went with haste to a Judean town in the hill country, where she entered the house of Zechariah and greeted Elizabeth. When Elizabeth heard Mary's greeting, the child leaped in her womb. And Elizabeth was filled with the Holy Spirit and exclaimed with a loud cry, "Blessed are you among women, and blessed is the fruit of your womb. And why has this happened to me, that the mother of my Lord comes to me? For as soon as I heard the sound of your greeting, the child in my womb leaped for joy. And blessed is she who believed that there would be a fulfillment of what was spoken to her by the Lord."

And Mary said,

"My soul magnifies the Lord,
    and my spirit rejoices in God my Savior,
for he has looked with favor on the lowliness of his servant.
    Surely, from now on all generations will call me blessed;
for the Mighty One has done great things for me,
    and holy is his name.
His mercy is for those who fear him
    from generation to generation.
He has shown strength with his arm;
    he has scattered the proud in the thoughts of their hearts.
He has brought down the powerful from their thrones,
    and lifted up the lowly;
he has filled the hungry with good things,
    and sent the rich away empty.
He has helped his servant Israel,
    in remembrance of his mercy,
according to the promise he made to our ancestors,
    to Abraham and to his descendants forever."

And Mary remained with her about three months and then returned to her home.

—Luke 1:39–56

CONNECTING WITH FRANCISCAN WRITINGS

Hail, holy Lady,
Most holy Queen,
Mary, Mother of God,
Ever Virgin;

Chosen by the most holy Father in heaven,
Consecrated by him,
With his most holy beloved Son
And the Holy Spirit, the Comforter.
On you descended and in you still remains
All the fullness of grace and every good.
Hail, his Palace.
Hail, his Tabernacle.
Hail, his Robe.
Hail, his Handmaid.
Hail, his Mother.
And Hail, all holy Virtues,
Who, by the grace
And inspiration of the Holy Spirit,
Are poured into the hearts of the faithful so that, faithless no
   longer,
They may be made faithful servants of God through you.

—St. Francis, "Salutation of the Blessed Virgin"

APPLICATION TO DAILY LIFE

- Mary's joys coexisted with suffering. Pray to find joy even in the sufferings and problems of daily life.
- Pray the Franciscan rosary at least once this week. Decide whether or not it will become a regular practice for you.

PRAYER

Holy Mary, Mother of God,
you trusted God with your whole life
when you said, "Let it be done to me."
Show us how to give birth to Jesus
in a world so in need of his love and forgiveness.
Amen.

········

PART TWO

Conversion

If we are to turn our lives to God, we must change. Change can be difficult and painful. Giving up old ways is challenging, especially when we have considered the way we've always done things to be right. The process of spiritual change is conversion. Conversion is not a once-and-for-all experience. Rather, it is something we do daily for the rest of our lives because, while we still breathe, we do not reach the spiritual perfection to which God calls us. The following reflections invite you to conversion again and again and again.

....

Turning to God and Away from Sin

"Fear God, love God, convert yourself from bad
to good."
    —St. Francis of Assisi, in Johannes Jorgensen's
                        St. Francis of Assisi

We can react in two ways to the beautiful truths we have
been studying. First, we can feel a deep sense of joy and
security in the fact that God our Father and mother loves us more
than any father and mother ever loved a child, that Christ our
brother continues his human-divine life in our human-graced life,
and that the Spirit of love dwells within us to be our strength, our
consolation, and our light.

We can respond, at the same time, with a frank and genuine
sense of sorrow for the indifference, selfishness, and sinful attitude
with which we have repaid God's love in the past. If we have not
turned completely away from God by mortal sinfulness, we have
been guilty of persistent attitudes of neglect and self-centeredness.
We have shown a certain unwillingness to love God "all the way."
Selfishness toward others has resulted.

Both attitudes, sorrow and joy, are part of the Christian virtue
of penance. Penance refers to a total turning to God by a basic
act of faith, sorrow, and love that becomes our way of life. This is
what our Lord was referring to in his first recorded public words:
"Repent, for the kingdom of heaven has come near (Matthew
4:17). Another name for this kind of penance is conversion. The
only way anyone can turn from evil and choose good is through
the deep realization of God's love that calls us to live so much in

the awareness of his loving presence that there is no appeal in evil for us, because it is not any part of God. In returning God's love, we can only choose the ways that are of God.

Francis speaks of a time when "he was still in sin." He is referring to the time of his life before he caught on to what the Christian life was all about. Like many others—indeed, it should happen to all of us—he went through a conversion. The word means a total turnaround, a complete giving of self to Christ, a conscious, all-out surrender to the grace of God.

It is immediately evident that one can have a conversion from a life of sin and estrangement to God—this would have been our Lord's first meaning—or from a superficial, rather thoughtless way of nominal Christian life.

We cannot judge anyone but ourselves. Many people may be deeply converted while appearing to lead what we think are rather ordinary lives, and some who are feverishly religious may not be deeply committed to Christ at all.

Christians baptized as babies sometimes grow into the faith so gradually that they never experience any one dramatic moment of conversion. Yet, they are indeed wholly converted to Christ. On the other hand, it is possible that someone may grow into the external practices of the faith without a deep and personal relationship to Christ. We must each look into our heart and face reality.

Each of us must admit that, while our love of God may be basic and fundamental, it is never whole. There is always an area of our life that we are afraid to give to God. The life of a Christian is a life of ongoing, never-ending conversion. There is, indeed, a once-and-for-all turning to God whereby we live in God's grace. Yet, we can all say with Francis, "Let us begin to do good, for as yet we have done nothing."

Ongoing conversion means letting the grace of God open us entirely to his will. We become free from every constraint except the gentle pressure of God's love. Every day we allow God to open us up, out of our narrowness and rigidity, to the freedom of his own life.

Conversion and ongoing conversion are referred to by these words of Christ, "If a man wishes to come after me, he must deny his very self, take up his cross, and begin to follow in my footsteps. Whoever would save his life will lose it, but whoever loses his life for my sake will find it." Self-denial here does not mean giving up candy during Lent. It means giving up every claim to our own will, every assertion of independence, every ounce of self-sufficiency. Conversion is a joyful-sorrowful rejection of all that cannot advance the glory of God and a peaceful acceptance of God's constant and gentle offer of friendship.

QUESTIONS FOR REFLECTION

- What does conversion mean in a Franciscan context?
- What is the most important aspect of penance, right now, in your life?

CONNECTING WITH SCRIPTURE

Then Jesus told his disciples, "If any want to become my followers, let them deny themselves and take up their cross and follow me. For those who want to save their life will lose it, and those who lose their life for my sake will find it. For what will it profit them if they gain the whole world but forfeit their life? Or what will they give in return for their life?

—Matthew 16:24–26

CONNECTING WITH FRANCISCAN WRITINGS

He had begun to feel lonely toward the end when the Dream was being challenged by so many of the brothers and when no one seemed to believe that the gospel life could in fact be lived in its entirety. Many brothers feared that the Rule of Life of the Lesser Brothers was too rigid, and they threatened to leave the brotherhood. Others were wandering about the countryside outside of obedience and some were even insulting Lady Poverty by constructing buildings for the brothers to live in. It was when this terrible weather was blowing through Francis' soul that the radiant spring of La Verna suddenly appeared.

The suffering face of Jesus had been deeply imprinted in his mind ever since that day in San Damiano when his Lord had spoken from the crucifix. All of his days from that time were spent in meditation on the suffering Christ and in being present to Jesus in His suffering. He wished with all his heart to stand beneath the cross of Christ, assuring Him of his love, that he would be there with Him, ever present on the hill of Calvary throughout the ages till the Risen Christ returned in all His glory and the cross would be no more!

It was with such an intention that Francis had made his final journey to the top of La Verna, that holy mountain far to the north of Assisi, La Verna, his mountain retreat. Even now in retrospect the miracle of La Verna filled his eyes with tears and his heart with affection and love for Jesus. There on that mountain, in preparation for the Feast of Saint Michael the Archangel, he had asked in fear and trembling that Christ would let him experience and share some of His suffering on the cross. What followed was more than a poor sparrow should or could expect.

—Murray Bodo, *Francis: The Journey and the Dream*

APPLICATION TO DAILY LIFE

- Was there a time or period in your life when you converted?
- How will there always be room for conversion in your life?
- In prayer this week, ask sincerely for your once-and-ongoing conversion.

PRAYER

Sometimes I do your will, Lord,
and I thank you for your guidance in those moments.
But, there are other times when I resist
and break away from you with selfish, willful stubbornness.
I am truly sorry for being less than you would have me be.
Change me, Lord, change me.
Amen.

The Consequences of Penance

"Francis, you must despise and hate all that your body has loved and desired up till now, if you would recognize my will. Once you have begun, you will find that everything which seemed pleasant and sweet to you will turn to unbearable bitterness, but the things that formerly made you shudder will give you peace and joy."
—adapted from Thomas of Celano, *Second Life of St. Francis*

Francis's Rule was comparatively mild in regards to fasting and other penitential practices. At the end of his life he apologized to his "Brother Body" for the harsh penance he had done. But the fact remains that Francis and his friars practiced severe penance.

Francis's words sound harsh to us today:

There are many people who, when they sin or are injured, frequently blame the enemy or their neighbor. But it is not so, because each one has the enemy in his power, that is his body through which he sins. Blessed is the servant, then, who always holds captive the enemy delivered into his power and wisely safeguards himself from him; because, as long as he does this, no other enemy visible or invisible will be able to harm him. (Admonition X)

St. Paul puts the matter this way: "I punish my body and enslave it, so that after proclaiming to others I myself should not be disqualified" (1 Corinthians 9:27).

Living in an affluent society, our culture seems to take for granted that pleasure, ease, and comfort are the be-all and end-all of life. Have we succumbed to a philosophy of hedonism, demanding everything that gratifies the body? We have all experienced the urge to excess, the tendency to a mindless and ungoverned grasping and gulping of pleasure, in food or drink or other things, or in imagination, emotion, anger, or the pursuit of whatever attracts us. At such a time as this, it is time to consider the age-old practice of fasting.

Christians know the earthly and eternal value of their bodies. Their self-denial is not a grim and prideful domineering of the body as a matter of personal achievement. Rather, it is the commonsense insurance against anything that threatens—and many dangers do threaten—their relationship with Christ.

This sort of penance is saying no when we need not, so that we can courageously say it when we must. Penance is a practiced yes to many good things that might have been left undone in preparation for the many moments when a joyous yes is the response God expects.

We are totally in debt to God whether sinners or just. God is the source of all goodness. We simply accept God's own healing of that which he has created.

Penance is a lifelong task, never finished. Penance is not a matter of gloom and discouragement, but of hope and confidence and joy tempered by a frank admission of past sins and present and future dangers.

QUESTIONS FOR REFLECTION

- Why does a Christian need to fast? And what do you particularly need to fast from?
- What does our faith add to the usual practice of asceticism? What makes it Christian?

CONNECTING WITH SCRIPTURE

Yet whatever gains I had, these I have come to regard as loss because of Christ. More than that, I regard everything as loss because of the surpassing value of knowing Christ Jesus my Lord. For his sake I have suffered the loss of all things, and I regard them as rubbish, in order that I may gain Christ and be found in him, not having a righteousness of my own that comes from the law, but one that comes through faith in Christ, the righteousness from God based on faith. I want to know Christ and the power of his resurrection and the sharing of his sufferings by becoming like him in his death, if somehow I may attain the resurrection from the dead.

—see Philippians 3:7–21

CONNECTING WITH FRANCISCAN WRITINGS

What brings one to penance and mortification? Is there any sense or reason behind renunciation and austerity? Why would anyone embrace the pain of separation as a way of life? Francis knew that people had these questions on their minds when they met the brothers. And especially did people wonder when men like Bernard of Quintavalle, the merchant, and Peter Catanii, the lawyer, left their professions and belongings behind and attached themselves to Francis.

To explain it was perhaps impossible, but it had something to do with restoring harmony within themselves and between themselves and their Creator. It was like a search for the Garden of Eden before the Fall. That Garden was the end of the Journey, and they of course knew it was not an attainable goal. Or was it? That was the question. In each of them there was the Dream of discovering within themselves a secret source of energy, a Presence that would transform their lives and restore the harmony of the Garden of Paradise.

So the pain of detachment was only a means of union. It was a way of stilling, of quieting everything that would prevent them from hearing that hushed knock of God within. That is why Francis had left his father. Pietro's world, his values and what he lived for, clamored so loud in Francis' ears, he could not hear the Voice in the heart of his real self. That is why he was willing and able to bear the insults and hooting of the citizens of Assisi; he heard a Voice within him that was even louder and more real than all the citizenry of the world. That is why he mortified his body when it clamored so loudly for attention that it threatened to drown out the peace of his Voice inside.

—Murray Bodo, *Francis: The Journey and the Dream*

APPLICATION TO DAILY LIFE

- What area in your life most needs discipline?
- What most needs atonement, reparation, and reconciliation?
- Will fasting be a part of your Franciscan spiritual practice this week?

PRAYER

Dear Jesus,
I know that fasting is emptying myself
so that your Spirit can fill me to overflowing.
Reveal to me what I must sacrifice for you—
food or drink, lust or gluttony, pride or pleasure-seeking,
judgmental nature or critical spirit.
Amen.

REFLECTION (14)

Reconciliation

"I feel that I am the greatest sinner that ever existed."

—St. Francis of Assisi

After Jesus made his fundamental demand to "repent and believe the Good News," he gave us a sign whereby we can be certain that God's power is within our repentance and that God's life becomes our new life. For Catholics, this is known as the sacrament of baptism.

A person may turn away from God even after being given this intimate relationship. But God always desires to bring us back to himself and to each other. When we destroy or disturb our relationship with God, there is an inevitable effect on our relationship with others, as well. We have only one spirit, and it affects everything we do. And if there is something sinful about our attitude toward others, this is at the same time an offense against God who has created and loves all of us. The two cannot be separated.

In fact, if there is something sinful in my attitude, no matter how secret I think it is, it has an effect on others. At its most simple level, I hurt others by not loving them as they have a right to be loved. Sin is never a private affair. Every sin is personal but has social ramifications.

Sin is expressed in external words and actions, especially by omissions. But sin goes much deeper. It brings disorder in our attitudes and value systems. Ultimately, sin affects our hearts, our inmost self. From there it touches and affects our relationships, our families, our world.

Each of us is unique. If the five people who know us inside out and backward were asked to describe us in two or three words, they would probably agree in substance: "happy-go-lucky," "perfectionist," "gives freely of herself," "quiet/withdrawn," "worrier/analyzer," and so on. Now it should be evident that our sinful attitude is going to be in the mold of our predominant characteristic.

Each of us should try to ferret out our predominant attitude or characteristic—it's evident to anyone who knows us—and see that it is the source of the sinfulness of our lives, no matter how varied its expression. This is what we bring back, time and again, to the forgiveness of Christ. Again and again we place our weakness within his strength, receive the assurance of his forgiveness and healing and continuing strength.

Our whole lives are an ongoing conversion, an attempt to open us up to God more and more. They are also a turning away from sinfulness—the infectious attitudes in us—over and over again. We do this in prayer, in the Eucharist, and in the sacrament that concentrates on our need for reconciliation and the ever-present willingness of God to give it.

QUESTIONS FOR REFLECTION

- How does all personal sin have social consequences?
- What is more to be worried about, the act or the attitude?

CONNECTING WITH SCRIPTURE

You have heard that it was said to those of ancient times, "You shall not murder'; and "whoever murders shall be liable to judgment." But I say to you that if you are angry with a brother or sister, you will be liable to judgment; and if you insult a brother or sister, you will be liable to the council; and if you say, "You fool," you will be liable to the hell of fire. So when you are offering your gift at the altar, if you remember that your brother or sister has something against you, leave your gift there before the altar and go; first be reconciled to your brother or sister, and then come and offer your gift. Come to terms quickly with your accuser while you are on the way to court with him, or your accuser may hand you over to the judge, and the judge to the guard, and you will be thrown into prison.

—Mathew 5:21–25

CONNECTING WITH FRANCISCAN WRITINGS

Francis knew that the hardest test of all would be to stand up to his strong-willed father. They were two of a kind, in a way, each bent stubbornly upon what he thought mattered most in life. For Pietro it was power and influence and the satisfaction of accomplishment in the world of business and trade. For Francis it had become weakness and littleness and poverty of spirit that paradoxically gave him power and influence and satisfaction of spirit. If he could not meet his father face to face and stand up to him, he would erase everything that had happened in the cave.

…

One day when Francis was begging in the streets and the crowd was unusually loud in its abuse, he passed his father's shop. Pietro was livid with shame and heartbreak. He ran from the shop, collared Francis and dragged him before the Bishop of Assisi. It was then that Jesus gave Francis the courage to meet his father.

Calmly, Francis stripped himself of his clothes; and placing them reverently at the feet of his father, he declared in a strong voice, "I have called Pietro Bernardone my father…. Now I will say Our Father who art in Heaven and not Pietro Bernardone." It was done, and Pietro realized he had gone too far with the boy. He wept inside for the son of his heart, but he would not make the first move toward reconciliation. What Francis had said was too final and too terrible to answer. The Bishop had covered Francis with his own cloak. And Francis left the court later that day clothed in a poor tunic that felt grander and more beautiful than all the finery in Assisi. The Dream had won.

—Murray Bodo, *Francis, The Journey and the Dream*

APPLICATION TO DAILY LIFE

- Do you think of the sacrament of reconciliation as a positive celebration of the mercy of God?
- Do you have a sense of your characteristic fault? Do you see it recurring again and again in your life?
- Spend part of your prayer time this week asking God's forgiveness for your sin.

PRAYER

I confess, Lord,
that I probably know my own unique, predominant fault
that leads me to sins of omission and commission;
but, too often, I deny that it is present in me.
Make me honest with myself and with you
so that I can offer this fault for your healing.
Amen.

The Poverty of Christ

"I, Brother Francis, wish to follow after the life and poverty of our highest Lord, Jesus Christ, and of his most holy mother, and I will hold out in this to the last."

—St. Francis of Assisi

First and before all, Francis wanted to imitate the poverty of Christ. He was not pursuing an abstract ideal. He saw the clear picture of the Gospels—a Christ who had nowhere to lay his head, and Francis responded, "Whatever he did, I want to do."

This fundamental lesson of Franciscan poverty must never be forgotten. Poverty, in the sense of nonpossession, is neither good nor bad—it is simply a fact. What makes Gospel poverty valuable is its purpose: the imitation of Christ for the purpose of Christ. This is why St. Paul's great hymn speaks of Jesus's "emptying" himself, foregoing the glory to which he had a right as God, entering into human nature in all its limitation, weakness, and suffering (Philippians 2:6–11).

By entering into the weakness and damages that sin had caused to us, Jesus could heal it by the holiness of his inner spirit. No matter what suffering he underwent, what frustration, misunderstanding, injustice, pain, deprivation, or poverty he endured, his human spirit was always directed in simple trust to the Father's praise. Francis had an intuition of the beauty of Christ's poverty. He wrote no profound philosophical analysis of this; he simply imitated it.

What was the result of Jesus entering into human poverty with a totally loving trust? He was able to enjoy all the things of earth that happened to come his way. He saw all creation as praising God, not as something to be grabbed, hidden, or sold. He saw all God's gifts as the inheritance of all people, to be shared in justice and charity. He saw all creation as the possession of everyone.

Jesus was the final flower of a movement that began in the Old Testament. At first, the poor were merely the miserable victims of society's greed and cruelty. As time went on, it came to be realized that since they were the victims of injustice, God had to be on their side. Their only trust was in God for the practical reason that there was no one else to go to. Gradually the poor became those who were totally dependent on God. They were those to whom God said, "Blessed are you poor." They did not put their trust in earthly things, whether they possessed them or not. The poorest of all these was the virgin of Nazareth. Because she was completely free of selfish attachments, completely open to God, Mary was the perfect virginal dwelling place in which the Word could "empty" himself into her spiritual and material poverty.

This was the vision of Francis, and this was the reason why he always joined Jesus and his mother in his praise of poverty.

We have still not settled the practical question as to whether poverty is material or spiritual, whether it is mainly positive or negative, whether it is an ascetical practice or a generous sharing of this world's goods with others. It is possible for a materially wealthy person to be totally unattached to his or her possessions. And a person poor in possessions can be stingy, grasping, and hoarding. If we place the question within the mystery of Christ, perhaps we can see that there is no neat answer.

QUESTIONS FOR REFLECTION

- What did Francis intend when he imitated the poverty of Christ?
- Who are the poor of today among whom the infant Jesus might be most comfortable?

CONNECTING WITH SCRIPTURE

Then the king will say to those at his right hand, "Come, you that are blessed by my Father, inherit the kingdom prepared for you from the foundation of the world; for I was hungry and you gave me food, I was thirsty and you gave me something to drink, I was a stranger and you welcomed me, I was naked and you gave me clothing, I was sick and you took care of me, I was in prison and you visited me." Then the righteous will answer him, "Lord, when was it that we saw you hungry and gave you food, or thirsty and gave you something to drink? And when was it that we saw you a stranger and welcomed you, or naked and gave you clothing? And when was it that we saw you sick or in prison and visited you?" And the king will answer them, "Truly I tell you, just as you did it to one of the least of these who are members of my family, you did it to me."

—see Matthew 25:31–46

CONNECTING WITH FRANCISCAN WRITINGS

Ownership may be a legal right, but possessiveness is a value, an attitude. Only when we live as poor persons do we recognize that the goods of this world do not belong to us and thus we may not possess them. Rather, they are gifts from God. To live in receptivity to the gift of God's goodness in creation is to live as a poor person, open to and dependent on the good of the human person, the good of the earth, and the good of the cosmos. When we claim the good as our own and refuse to share the goods of our lives, we miss the mark of God's justice; this is sin.

—Ilia Delio, *Compassion*

APPLICATION TO DAILY LIFE

- How does the spirit of Gospel poverty apply to buying a car, a home, or entertainment? How does it enter into the raising of children?
- Is it possible to be "Gospel poor" in our affluent society?
- Try, this week, deliberately sharing some valuable possession with another person in a new way.

PRAYER

Lord, show me how to be poor
in a culture that worships the wealth
of power, possessions, and prestige.
Amen.

Poverty for the Kingdom

"Once, when he [St. Francis] was returning from
Siena, he met a beggar and said to his companion,
'We must give back to the poor little man the cape
that belongs to him, for we have only received it
as a loan until we meet someone who is poorer
than we.'"

—*The Writings of Brother Leo*

Poverty, both rightly and wrongly understood, has been the
badge of Francis and his Order from the beginning. He
is known as the "poor little man of Assisi." His first Rule was
largely a collection of Scripture texts on poverty. The crises in the
Order, even during the life of Francis, hinged on the interpretation
of Gospel poverty. The ideal and practice of poverty are still
challenging and perplexing for Franciscans today.

The problem of poverty has three parts: (1) What kind of
poverty is Jesus talking about? Luke's Gospel says, "Blessed
are you poor." Matthew's Gospel says, "Blessed are the poor in
spirit." Are we called to material or spiritual poverty? Can they
be separated? (2) Is poverty primarily a not-having, a form of
asceticism and purification, or does it have a more important
and positive orientation? (3) Is poverty an inward-looking virtue,
something primarily concerned with the holiness of those who
practice it, or is its real purpose the sharing of earthly goods with
others?

Whatever else Gospel poverty is, it is an attack on the root of
all evil, greed. But money is neither good nor bad in itself. Money

can buy medicine for a friend or poison for an enemy. Not having money can produce saints or criminals. The virtue of Gospel poverty frees us from an unreasonable or slavish attachment to things. The Holy Spirit has told us that the love of money is the root of all evil (1 Timothy 6:10). Therefore, in the logic of St. Bonaventure, detachment from an unreasonable love of money must be the root of all good. It is the enslavement to money that is evil. Money can buy pleasure, prestige, and power. These can become insatiable—the more I get, the more I want. So, for all Christians, the virtue of Gospel poverty is necessary to curb and control this basic danger in our weakened human nature.

At a discussion of religious poverty, one participant made a telling remark, "Look, to be poor means not to have access to power. As long as we have power, let's not say we are practicing 'poverty!'" Gospel poverty, it would seem, must have some effect on the material things we have and use. At the very least, it calls for a sparing use of things, both as ascetical practice and as a means of sharing our goods with others.

The problem will not be solved by a blueprint of observances. The answer can only come from a more basic question: How will someone act in regard to his money and possessions once the love of Christ has possessed his heart and he sees the whole world as God's gift and all people as his brothers and sisters?

Let us never forget the purpose of the virtue, which is freedom to love God. The Bible speaks of "the freedom of the children of God," and Christ said, "If you continue in my word, you are truly my disciples; and you will know the truth, and the truth will make you free" (John 8:31–32). Freedom negatively means the absence of slavery to sin, death, and the devil. Positively, freedom means the power to be like God by our choices. The danger to humanity is that it becomes enslaved by the physical pleasures of the body and the selfish pleasures of pride and self-love. Poverty is designed to make us free of any enslavement to things and to persons, places, circumstances, and desires. Francis saw the danger of being attached to anyone or anything to the degree that perfect love of God would become difficult or even impossible.

The social and economic situation in the world today makes it impossible to divorce any discussion of Gospel poverty from a Christian concern for justice for the poor and deprived—both individuals and nations. Francis felt that anything he had or used was on loan from God, to be held in stewardship until someone poorer than he came along. He was always giving away his cloak to beggars. He gave away the only copy of the New Testament the friars had so that a poor woman could buy bread.

A modern spiritual writer has suggested that the vow of poverty be renamed. He suggested "generous sharing" instead. Indeed, such an emphasis will save the practice of poverty from being a sterile, self-conscious, and introverted practice that does no more than flatter the pride of the practitioner. Charity to others for the love of God is the primary virtue. To be poor before God is to be totally open to his gifts and then totally open to the needs of others—for whose sake the gifts are given to us.

Therefore, to live like Francis, we ask: "What can I do every day, within the actual circumstances and obligations of my life, to cut any creeping enslavement to money or possessions? What will make me free? What needs of others can I fulfill with my monetary support or outright gift?" Like Francis, we have no rules for this. As he said, "The Lord showed me what to do."

QUESTIONS FOR REFLECTION

- From what does the spirit of poverty free us?
- What does the spirit of poverty produce in us?
- What is poverty?

CONNECTING WITH SCRIPTURE

He sat down opposite the treasury, and watched the crowd putting money into the treasury. Many rich people put in large sums. A poor widow came and put in two small copper coins, which are worth a penny. Then he called his disciples and said to them, "Truly I tell you, this poor widow has put in more than all those who are contributing to the treasury. For all of them have contributed out of their abundance; but she out of her poverty has put in everything she had, all she had to live on."

—Mark 12:41–44

CONNECTING WITH FRANCISCAN WRITINGS

One day when Francis was busily preoccupied with a fat and wealthy matron, a beggar sidled up to him and butted rudely into the conversation. Francis, offended both by the rudeness and by the dirty appearance of the man, curtly dismissed him and turned back to the woman. The beggar, surprised by this kind of treatment from the reputedly generous Francis, grumbled and cursed and left the shop in a huff, spitting on the cobblestones in front of the store.... Years later Francis told Brother Leo this incident and added, "Brother Leo, I felt so small that day. If the beggar had asked for alms in the name of some count, I would have asked the woman to excuse me for a minute and I would have given the man a handsome sum.

"But, instead, I resented this uncouth behavior when I was talking to an important lady. But when he left, all I could hear drumming in my ears was the remark with which the beggar prefaced his request, 'For the love of God.' That was the first time, Brother Leo, that I realized I had been generous in order to win human praise and so that I would ingratiate myself with people. But the love of God I was willing to postpone until after an important business deal. The revelation was like an epiphany, a shining, glorious revelation from God. It hit me immediately and deeply and put my mind in a spin until I couldn't stand it any longer and ran from the shop after the still disgruntled beggar. How stunned he was when I caught up with him and literally poured the gold coins into his shaking palms. It was the first time that I really felt free and close to God."

—Murray Bodo, *Francis: The Journey and the Dream*

APPLICATION TO DAILY LIFE

- What evidences of slavish attachment to things, arrangements, and comforts can you find in your life?
- Can a rich woman be poor? Can a poor man be greedy?
- Try to uncover greed in your life this week. Deny yourself something and give it to God through others.

PRAYER

"Thy kingdom come, thy will be done"—
with my time, my possessions, my talents,
my bank account, my wages, my love, my...
Amen.

REFLECTION (17)

Some External Applications of Poverty

> Witnessing to the good yet to come and obliged
> to acquire purity of heart because of the vocation
> they have embraced, they should set themselves
> free to love God and their brothers and sisters.
> The "spirit of poverty" is the attitude of being
> free, not enslaved by money and what money can
> buy. We are not discontented with the limitations
> that our lack of money imposes upon us. We try
> to live our lives with the things we really need,
> instead of letting our desires control our life.
> Franciscan poverty flees from luxury and loves
> the things that give less pleasure to the ego and
> to vanity.
>
> —Rule of the Secular Franciscan Order, 12

Fallen human nature hates restraint. It thinks that happiness consists in freely doing whatever pleases passion or pride. But Christ says we are free if we love God and are not the slaves of sin. In other words, if we deny ourselves and say "yes!" to God, we are free. We are free from all harm and free to accept the happiness God offers us.

Poverty sees the good in ordinary things. We are not told to "put up with" or "grimly suffer" things that give less pleasure. We are to be cheerful, glad, and perfectly willing not to have the latest car, the fanciest clothing, or the expensive house. There is nothing wrong with what pleases the eye. The danger is in the vanity, the conceit, the greed that often lurks beneath. Practicing poverty keeps us from becoming slaves to pleasure, prestige, or power.

We have a hundred chances a day to break the accumulative habit that wants to dominate our lives, enslaving us to things instead of making things serve us. Franciscan poverty calls us to avoid vanity in appearance and clothes and adhere to the standard of simplicity, moderation, and propriety that benefits us.

Our society is characterized by impulse-buying and consumerism. Perhaps never before in history have people indulged in such wasteful buying of luxuries, duplicates, and gadgets. But Gospel poverty is not mere thrift. Still less is it miserliness. Gospel poverty is a clear decision to use God's gifts with reason. It does not try to maintain a posture. Gospel poverty does not deny self or children necessary or reasonable things, but neither does it buy prestige.

QUESTIONS FOR REFLECTION

- What separates Gospel poverty from miserliness? From the grinding poverty of injustice?
- How might a Franciscan commitment to poverty affect our purchase of a car? A home? The latest technological gadget?

CONNECTING WITH SCRIPTURE

Now the whole group of those who believed were of one heart and soul, and no one claimed private ownership of any possessions, but everything they owned was held in common. With great power the apostles gave their testimony to the resurrection of the Lord Jesus, and great grace was upon them all. There was not a needy person among them, for as many as owned lands or houses sold them and brought the proceeds of what was sold. They laid it at the apostles' feet, and it was distributed to each as any had need. There was a Levite, a native of Cyprus, Joseph, to whom the apostles gave the name Barnabas (which means "son of encouragement"). He sold a field that belonged to him, then brought the money, and laid it at the apostles' feet.

—Acts 4:32–37

CONNECTING WITH FRANCISCAN WRITINGS

Francis smiled now at his absolute seriousness as he stood before his parents, fully clad in hauberk and surcoat, chausses of banded mail, helm and buckler, belt and sword. He truly must have been impressive to behold, yes, and a little stiff and awkward, too. How important he felt and how silly it all seemed now. Could anyone be less free than an armored man? And yet, at the time, it was all perfectly marvelous. What pain and discomfort people endure to look important.

That moment, as he stood in front of his admiring parents, had a further significance for Francis. It was possibly the only time in his life that he pleased both his mother and his father simultaneously. He was to enter the service of Pope Innocent and therefore to his mother he was truly a man of God. And he looked truly like Lancelot himself, so to his father, he was the most impressive soldier to ride out of Assisi in years.

The Dream at Spoleto dashed all of that. And he came home a disappointment to his father and a worry to his mother. For he began then the shedding of armor and mail, and it literally took years to shed the last of that confining metal and emerge a free man of flesh and spirit. And ever and again the temptation returned to put on more clothes, to confine himself and constrict his spirit with material things.

Once, years later, someone gave him a lovely little basket. But when he tried to pray, he could not keep his mind on God for thinking of the delicate and beautiful basket. So Francis left his cave and went out and burned the basket. When he returned, his mind and heart soared once again to his Father in Heaven. Some of the brothers said he should have given the basket to someone or sold it and given the money to the poor, but at that moment an immolation seemed called for, and in burning it, he had given it to God. Besides, those brothers had never worn armor, and they couldn't have known how cumbersome armor was and how useless it was to the spirit.

—Murray Bodo, *Francis: The Journey and the Dream*

APPLICATION TO DAILY LIFE

- Is living with a commitment to Franciscan poverty easy or difficult for you? Why?
- Try this week to practice "a certain sparingness" in food and drink and to give what you save to a charitable cause.

PRAYER

Free me, Lord, from the bondage of too much.
Unclutter my life from the tyranny of things.
Lead me on the path of simple living.
Amen.

··

Humility: The Twin of Poverty

"A man is what he is in the sight of God, and
nothing more. If the Lord should take from me
his treasure, which he has loaned me, what else
would remain to me except a body and soul, no
different from that of the infidels?"

—St. Francis of Assisi

In his simple wisdom, Francis saw poverty and humility as
twins. We are absolutely dependent on God for all things: that
is humility. And God will provide them: that is poverty. We are
nothing without God: that is humility. We want nothing but God:
that is poverty. As creatures, we are poor before God: that is both
poverty and humility. Humility is a virtue whereby we realize
and act according to our nothingness apart from God and our
complete dependence upon God.

Christ began his Sermon on the Mount with the Beatitudes.
First among them is "Blessed are the poor in spirit" (Matthew
5:3). This has two meanings: (1) How happy are they who are free
because of their spirit of Gospel poverty, and (2) how happy are
they who realize and admit that they are absolutely poor before
God and thus see everything as a gift!

The fundamental statement of humility was made by our Lord.
"Those who abide in me and I in them bear much fruit, because
apart from me you can do nothing" (John 15:5).

Nothing can exist without God. Our hearts will not beat
another beat, our next breath will not be drawn unless God keeps
on maintaining our lives. We cannot raise a finger a fraction of an
inch or love our neighbor unless God keeps us alive. Humility is,

therefore, a deep and simple virtue. It acknowledges our absolute nothingness without God and our complete dependence on God every second of every day. "Not that we are competent of ourselves to claim anything as coming from us; our competence is from God" (2 Corinthians 3:5). It is hard for proud human beings to believe this basic truth of all life.

Humility in this sense was in Christ. His human nature was as dependent on the divine as we are. Therefore, Jesus had to say: "I do nothing on my own, but I speak these things as the Father instructed me. And the one who sent me is with me; he has not left me alone, for I always do what is pleasing to him" (John 8:28–29). Mary, in all her immaculate beauty of soul, had to say, "Here am I, the servant of the Lord; let it be with me according to your word" (Luke 1:38). She was nothing without God. How much more we ought to recognize this Christ as our model in humility. Just as he depended on his Father, so we must depend on God.

One of the greatest tragedies of life is the self-hate or the lack of a sense of self-worth that afflicts many people—sometimes without their realizing it. They feel completely insecure. How can anyone love them since they are not worth loving? How can they love others since they have nothing to give? How can they believe that others really love them since they are nothing?

This attitude does not reflect humility but emotional sickness, the terrible result of others' lack of love. Anyone who is truly humble before God has heard the Good News, that God has made us really something—his children. And God loves us!

Pride, humility's opposite, is the infected heart of all sin. It says, "I am somebody, all by myself. I am independent, worthwhile, all by myself. I need no one, not even God."

The tragedy of so many good people is the infection of pride that runs through their whole lives. One can be proud of the holiest things such as prayer and kindness. One can even be proud of humility!

Francis always mentioned humility in the same breath with poverty. In a sense, they are the same: personally doing without. This is a fact, because all that we have is from God. This is an ideal, because we want to be without everything but God. Some of the most striking things Francis said concern humility: "A man is what he is in the sight of God and nothing more." "The better a man really is, the worse he feels himself to be." The more we appreciate God's gifts and unending generosity, the more we become conscious of refusing to admit this and spoiling God's precious gifts. As with St. Paul, the only thing Francis would take pride in was the "cross of Christ."

Even while he was the happiest of men, Francis felt himself to be the worst sinner in the world. No one ever took more seriously Christ's words, "When you have done all you have been commanded, say, 'We are worthless slaves; we have done only what we ought to have done'" (Luke 17:10). The follower of Christ was trying to keep a balance: realizing his nothingness but believing in God's love.

QUESTIONS FOR REFLECTION

• What words best describe the ingredients of humility?
• What is the worst sin of all?

CONNECTING WITH SCRIPTURE

The apostles said to the Lord, "Increase our faith!" The Lord replied, "If you had faith the size of a mustard seed, you could say to this mulberry tree, 'Be uprooted and planted in the sea,' and it would obey you.

"Who among you would say to your slave who has just come in from ploughing or tending sheep in the field, 'Come here at

once and take your place at the table'? Would you not rather say
to him, 'Prepare supper for me, put on your apron and serve me
while I eat and drink; later you may eat and drink'? Do you thank
the slave for doing what was commanded? So you also, when you
have done all that you were ordered to do, say, 'We are worthless
slaves; we have done only what we ought to have done!'"

—Luke 17:1–10

CONNECTING WITH FRANCISCAN WRITINGS

In a picture of our Lord or the Blessed Virgin painted on wood,
our Lord and the Blessed Virgin are honored, and yet the wood
and the painting ascribe nothing of it to themselves. So the servant
of God is a kind of painting of God in which God is honored. But
the servant ought to attribute nothing to himself. In comparison
with God he is even less than wood or painting. Indeed he is pure
nothing.

—St. Francis, *The Mirror of Perfection*

APPLICATION TO DAILY LIFE

- What things do you like to think you can do without God's
  help?
- Which saying of Francis on humility strikes you most forcibly?
- Take time this week to credit God for the talents you have and
  the good you do. Likewise, take responsibility for the evil you
  find in yourself.

PRAYER

"Of myself I can do nothing."
I praise you and thank you, my Creator,
for what you choose to do in and through me.
Amen.

REFLECTION (19)

Humility toward Others

"I admonish and exhort them [the friars] not to despise or judge people they see dressed in soft and showy garments and using choice food or drink, but rather let each one judge and despise himself."

—St. Francis of Assisi

If we are humble before God, we cannot be conceited before others. Humility recognizes the great truth: Everything is from God. If everything is God's, what point is there in comparison? Is God jealous of himself? He gives this man or woman this or that talent, money, honor, status. He has given me perhaps more, perhaps less. What's the difference? It's all God's! Shall I be unhappy because God has given a gift to another? To Francis, living the Gospel life meant charity, not judging. He was not worried about measuring his gifts against those of others. He simply wanted to give everybody as much of God's treasure as possible. If God gives us a gift which he did not give to another, he did it for just one reason: that we produce fruit with it.

What do we know of what others are like on the inside? If someone seems to be bad, what do we know of his past experiences, parents, home life, education, temptations, emotions, the bad influences he has suffered, the cruelty or deception inflicted on him, the ignorance, pain, physical or mental sickness, worry, misunderstanding that have entered his life? Who but God knows the human heart? Even when someone seems to be evil—deliberately so, bragging of it—we still have the principle of St. Bonaventure: "I must consider myself below others, not because I am certain that I am, but because I am more certain of my unworthiness than I am of theirs." We can only appreciate our own toothache—and our own sin.

Francis had a horror of seeming better than he was. He told his friars, after an act of charity, that he was tempted to be vain. On Easter Sunday he got up before the people and made known that he had eaten chicken during Lent (as the doctor had ordered him). When his health required wearing warmer clothing, a fox-pelt over his stomach, he insisted that one be sewn on the outside also so that everyone would see how self-indulgent he was. At night he would pretend to sleep and later rise when he thought no one was watching to spend long hours in prayer.

Humility was in the very name Francis gave his friars: the Friars Minor or "lesser brothers." The minors of his day were the same as they are now—the little people, noble only in their goodness, not particularly distinguished in the eyes of the world. We may be high in the world of business, art, or science, and may be endowed with great talents of mind, body, or grace, but in the spirit of Francis, we must fight against the infection of pride and the alluring temptation to act only to impress others and draw their flattery. We should remember that we are very little—in fact, nothing of ourselves. Pride is the sin within all sins.

QUESTIONS FOR REFLECTION

- What is the answer to the temptation to compare yourself with others?
- Who are minors today in the Franciscan sense? How can you make yourself like them?

CONNECTING WITH SCRIPTURE

Do not judge, so that you may not be judged. For with the judgment you make you will be judged, and the measure you give will be the measure you get. Why do you see the speck in your neighbor's eye, but do not notice the log in your own eye? Or how can you say to your neighbor, "Let me take the speck out of your eye," while the log is in your own eye? You hypocrite, first take the log out of your own eye, and then you will see clearly to take the speck out of your neighbor's eye.

—Matthew 7:1–5

CONNECTING WITH FRANCISCAN WRITINGS

Brother Masseo once said to Francis:

"I wonder why the whole world runs after you! You are not handsome; you are not deeply learned; you are not of noble birth!" Francis said, "Do you wish to know? I know the answer from the all-seeing God, whose eyes see the good and the bad all over the earth. For those most holy eyes have nowhere seen a greater, more miserable, poorer sinner than I; because in all the earth he has found no more wretched being to do his wonderful work. Therefore, he has chosen me, so as to put to shame the noble and the great, that all may know that all power and virtue come from him, and not from creatures, and no one can exalt himself before his face."

—*The Little Flowers of St. Francis*

APPLICATION TO DAILY LIFE

• If you have twice as much talent from God (in homemaking, computer skills, music, art, strength) as another, what does God expect?

• In what area of God's gifts do you tend to think you are better than others (by your own efforts, of course)?

• Try this week not to go about proving yourself to anyone ever, but to repeatedly say with Francis, "There, but for the grace of God, go I!"

PRAYER

I will try to remember, Lord,
that your Spirit lives in each person I meet—
the proud and the downtrodden,
the beautiful and the homely,
the wise and the ignorant,
the good and the not so good.
Keep me mindful that at times I may be like each of them.
Amen.

REFLECTION (20)

Chastity: Respect for Self and Others

"It was impossible to say anything really bad about Francis. In all that related to the other sex he was a model. It was known among his friends that no one dare say an evil word in his hearing. If it happened, at once his face assumed a serious, almost harsh, expression, and he did not answer. Like all the pure of heart, Francis had great reverence for the mysteries of life."

— Johannes Jorgensen, *St. Francis of Assisi*

Sexuality is an inseparable element of human life. As God made us, sexuality is coextensive with human life. It should not be considered primarily or solely in terms of intercourse (genital sexuality) or marriage. These are not its only manifestations. Some people may never marry, never procreate, yet they remain as fully sexual as those who do. They live in loving relationships as this particular man or this individual woman.

Chastity is a virtue (habit, attitude, ongoing practice) that reverences and orders sexuality according to God's will. In marriage, it integrates the full use and enjoyment of sexual powers with the unselfish and reverential relationship of love between husband and wife. In the single life, as celibacy, it moderates and guides a man's or woman's life as a sexual person while abstaining from genital sexuality. In either case, it is respect, born of faith, for all persons as temples of the Holy Spirit.

The positive emphasis on the healthiness and holiness of sexuality may be said to have started on the first page of the Bible.

"Male and female he created them...and God saw that it was good." The obvious meaning of sexuality is that all human beings need each other.

What is more, God himself was made flesh, had sexuality. If we didn't catch the goodness from the fact of creation, we certainly can't miss it from the fact that Jesus was a fully human male—something for all believers in the Incarnation to ponder.

We can never lose sight of the fact that every human being is sacred to God, purchased by the blood of Christ, hovered over by the Spirit. The whole person, inseparably body and spirit, is sacred. I may not use or abuse any person's mind, talents, emotions, or body for my selfish purposes. Whether for sexual, materialistic, or intellectual gratification, I may never see another person as a thing.

The spirit of chastity, like that of poverty, is a quest for and a preservation of freedom. Those whose sexuality is aligned with God's will are truly free. They use God's gift according to the relationships into which he has put them. They do not let themselves be enslaved to anyone or anything but God.

QUESTIONS FOR REFLECTION

- What does chastity mean? What is celibacy?
- Why did God make us sexual?

CONNECTING WITH SCRIPTURE

Then the Lord God said, "It is not good that the man should be alone; I will make him a helper as his partner." So out of the ground the Lord God formed every animal of the field and every bird of the air, and brought them to the man to see what he would call them; and whatever the man called each living creature, that was its name. The man gave names to all cattle, and to the birds of the air, and to every animal of the field; but for the man there was not found a helper as his partner. So the Lord God caused a deep sleep to fall upon the man, and he slept; then he took one of his ribs and closed up its place with flesh. And the rib that the Lord God had taken from the man he made into a woman and brought her to the man. Then the man said,

"This at last is bone of my bones
and flesh of my flesh;
this one shall be called Woman,
for out of Man this one was taken."

Therefore a man leaves his father and his mother and clings to his wife, and they become one flesh. And the man and his wife were both naked, and were not ashamed.

—Genesis 2:15–25

CONNECTING WITH FRANCISCAN WRITINGS

To speak of love had never been difficult for Francis until Christ stole his heart. Then there was something so sacred about their relationship that all love became love caught up in Jesus. When he heard the Gospel read at Mass, it was Jesus speaking directly to him, and every word was a love-word. He swallowed each word and assimilated it into his whole being. He wanted to become one with the Word, to make literally his own the Word of God. This Word of God was its own message, because Jesus was the Word and by becoming a man he had put flesh onto His own message of love.

He was the Word. So when Francis heard the Gospels read aloud, it was as if Jesus Himself were entering his ears and filling his whole self with His presence. And the word he listened to took on flesh in Francis himself.

…

So celibacy for Francis was not something sterile and barren, and he never thought of celibacy anyway, but of virginity, which was more positive and implied something you chose for the

Kingdom rather than something you endured because of your role in the church. Virginity brought fullness to Francis because, in renouncing marriage, he did not shrink as a person but grew in his capacity to love more and more people. He moved in a world much larger than the family.

Besides, his identification with Jesus was so absolute and literal that he could never be anything other than a virgin like Christ. Francis thought that Jesus' own virginity made possible His total love for him, and vice versa. And the paradox in Francis' life was that his exclusive love for Jesus was at the same time inclusive of all humanity. Again what he had renounced had come rushing down in waterfalls of new capacities for love and giving. And the pool of self was constantly refilled with the fresh and clean water of love that flowed out of Francis in countless streams of attention, affection, and service of others. The living waters of Jesus had become his own, and he thereby became a reservoir of unselfish love for all creatures.

—Murray Bodo, *Francis: The Journey and the Dream*

APPLICATION TO DAILY LIFE

- If you are married, how can you increase your respect for your partner and thus ensure the full and God-given enjoyment of marriage?
- In prayer this week, meditate on the wholeness and healthiness of your life. Ask for increased commitment to others in your relationships.

PRAYER

Lord, show me how chastity means
reserving the best of myself for you
while sharing the best of you with others.
Amen.

REFLECTION (21)

Setting a Good Example

"Set the believers an example in speech and
conduct, in love, in faith, in purity."

—1 Timothy 4:12

Whether we like it or not, the world is upon us like a flood.
Electronics and technology unimaginable a decade ago are
probably the best symbols of what has happened. Almost without
thinking, we see events around the world. We communicate with
people everywhere instantaneously.

We are part of a people who are called individually and as
a community to be the body of Christ. We have the power to
answer that call courageously and faithfully. We have the holiness
and power of Christ's own spirit within. We can answer the call to
"glorify God and bear him in your bodies." We can be a powerful
witness in the worst of circumstances to the presence of Christ.
Our unselfishness, respect for others, desire for material things,
the good works we do to make others' lives better, our reverence
for our own bodies, and those of others as part of our whole
Christian commitment speak to every person we meet. They may
not admit it. They may ridicule it in embarrassment. They may
react in anger, but they cannot fail to get the message.

Young people learn from the time they are born by experiencing
the love of good parents, learning unselfishness, respect, concern,
and responsibility. Before marriage or single life can be successful,
individuals must learn to live for others, not just themselves.
They can find joy in using their creativity and energy in athletic
endeavors, music, art, work projects in poor areas of their city,

visiting the lonely elderly in nursing homes. Such activities create wholesome lifestyles. Self-esteem grows as young people discover their gifts from God that they can use to make the world a better place.

The place of the physical in life is part of that learning. When we're young, we learn to accept our sexuality as a beautiful and essential part of our personalities, but not as the sole way of expressing our vitality. We too easily observe lives wrecked by a false sense of values. And by the grace of God, we choose a life of devotion to Christ in which we are fully sexual, always trying to become more open and mature. We learn that possessing material goods does not ensure happiness.

QUESTIONS FOR REFLECTION

- What are some of the ways that kids learned what was right and good when you were growing up?
- From what you know of St. Francis, to whom did he look to for a good Christian example?

CONNECTING WITH SCRIPTURE

I appeal to you therefore, brothers and sisters, by the mercies of God, to present your bodies as a living sacrifice, holy and acceptable to God, which is your spiritual worship. Do not be conformed to this world, but be transformed by the renewing of your minds, so that you may discern what is the will of God—what is good and acceptable and perfect.

—Romans 12:1–2

CONNECTING WITH FRANCISCAN WRITINGS

Glancing over his shoulder as he left the piazza, Francis noticed a knight sitting on a great charger and talking to a young boy who was obviously in awe of the gallant man in his polished armor and doublet of deep scarlet. All the memories rushed in. He saw himself in the little open-mouthed boy, and he remembered his fascination at the knights who rode into the piazzas of Assisi with the clatter of horse and the ring of metal clacking in the air. He would rush from his father's shop and up the little incline to the Piazza Commune and stand staring in wonder at so glorious a sight.

The knight represented everything he had wanted to become. Courageous, yet courteous and kind; a feared foe in the field and yet a genteel protector of the weak and helpless; fierce in the face of evil, yet gentle and handsome before the ladies. And then he had gone to war in one of the countless skirmishes between Assisi and Perugia, the powerful neighbor to the north. He rode out of Assisi with the seriousness of Charlemagne himself, and he could see out of the corner of his fixed, determined eyes that the young boys of Assisi flushed with pride as he passed.

But all that pomp and ceremony was dashed to the ground at Ponte San Giovanni where the army of Assisi was defeated and Francis himself taken prisoner. There at the bridge halfway between Assisi and Perugia he saw for the first time the real face of war, and it was ugly and plain, and there was no glory in it, even for the victor. And yet, so strong was the call of chivalry and honor that after a year's imprisonment in Perugia and a long illness at home, he set out again with the forces of Walter of Brienne. He did not, however, have to see the squalor of war once again because at Spoleto, only a short ride from Assisi, he had the Vision, the Dream that changed his life. And all his life from that moment on, his heart was turned away from making war to making peace.

The same virtues were there: courage and courtesy, chivalry and adventure, honor and fierceness of purpose. But now it was not in war that they were tested but in the battle inside the human heart.

Francis saw that the real battle was inside, and if that battle could be won, the call to arms would no longer be necessary. He did not know if that was possible; he only tried to make it come true in his own heart and hope that others would follow his example.

He had begun to think small instead of big, to start with himself instead of with forces and people outside. And he prayed that someday that little boy in the piazza would stand open-mouthed and flushed with excitement to see a barefoot beggar walk across the square with eyes that flashed with victory and ragged clothes that shone with the radiance of purity and poverty of spirit.

—Murray Bodo, *Francis: The Journey and the Dream*

APPLICATION TO DAILY LIFE

- What virtues did Francis emulate as a child in worldly ways, only to discover them more profoundly later as a follower of Christ?
- Pray this week for the grace to be respectful of yourself and others.

PRAYER

O, God, guide me in a way of life
that will reveal to young people I meet
the joy of living in your Spirit.
Fill me with true love rather than lust,
desire to serve you rather than myself,
and the courage to live by your laws
rather than the world's temptations.
Amen.

Obedience

> "The Rule and Life of the Lesser Brothers is this: to observe the Holy Gospel of Our Lord Jesus Christ by living in obedience, without anything of one's own, and in chastity.
>
> "Brother Francis promises obedience and reverence to our Lord Pope Honorius and his successors canonically elected and to the Roman Church. Let the other brothers be bound to obey Brother Francis and his successors."
>
> —St. Francis of Assisi, *The Later Rule*

The whole world suffers an authority crisis. Partly because of the instantaneous and detailed broadcasting of all the faults of authority, partly because of a greater sense of the value and freedom of each individual, it is difficult for anyone in authority to have credibility and influence. This points to a great need for responsible people to lead the way in sincere and respectful cooperation with authority.

At the same time, one need not be mindless or thoughtless to be obedient. A healthy, honest expression of opinion is welcomed by any mature person in authority. No one is all-wise. We need each other's ideas, encouragement, and just criticism. We learn from them. We grow from them.

Followers of Francis should try to have the "obedience of charity" so much praised by him. Obedience possesses two grace-filled purposes. First, obedience provides a means of self-denial and self-giving. Obedience seeks freedom from all stubbornness, selfishness, and self-centeredness. Obedience calls one to exercise self-discipline. This effort will have one great result: release from self-seeking and pride.

Second, obedience of vow or spirit is to realize that it means "giving oneself to the cause." This cause is the Church's mission to live and preach the Gospel. By obedience we make ourselves available to the Church for whatever she might call us to perform.

Francis himself had little knack for organization. He was a free spirit, guided by the Spirit of God, drawing men (and then women) to follow him by the sheer force of his Gospel life. He thought in terms of spirit rather than law, the burning urgency of inspired Christians rather than the more prosaic caution of experience. But he himself recognized that thousands of Franciscans could no longer live according to a few simple rules. Something was needed to keep some order in the Franciscan household. Thus, he rewrote the Rule as the situation demanded. Francis wisely submitted his movement to the guidance of the Church. The few Gospel texts that had been the foundation of the early life of the Order gave way to more structure.

At the core of the Christian life is Jesus Christ, manifested by the Body of Christ as he exists among his people. Followers of Francis are gathered by the Spirit as a body of people called together by God to live a Gospel life of prayer and service. It is a group of people who share a vision of a new life, who care for each other in their needs, who form a place where God dwells, a joyous and prayerful people who are sent forth to build the Lord's Kingdom.

A certain independence of thought and action is characteristic of the Franciscan way. Francis himself broke out of the medieval mold. At the same time, Francis was in touch with the Holy Spirit and recognized the Holy Father as God's voice to him. There is always an appropriate balance between independence and authority. Obedience then becomes free and wholehearted cooperation with the decisions of the shepherds of the Church. Francis was described soon after his death as a "wholly catholic and apostolic man."

QUESTIONS FOR REFLECTION
- How does obedience compare with poverty and chastity?
- What two purposes can obedience have?

CONNECTING WITH SCRIPTURE
When the ten heard this, they began to be angry with James and John. So Jesus called them and said to them, "You know that among the Gentiles those whom they recognize as their rulers lord it over them, and their great ones are tyrants over them. But it is not so among you; but whoever wishes to become great among you must be your servant, and whoever wishes to be first among you must be slave of all. For the Son of Man came not to be served but to serve, and to give his life a ransom for many."

—Mark 10:41–45

CONNECTING WITH FRANCISCAN WRITINGS
Francis perceived that the will's self-centeredness can be transformed only by being other-centered. The virtue of obedience can be a means of transformation because obedience requires a listening to another and letting go of our wills out of love for one another. Obedience does not necessarily entail having a superior, commanding officer or a demanding parent. Rather, obedience can take place between friends, lovers, family or in community. Obedience does not mean a hierarchy of order, a top-down chain of command, but a relationship of mutuality whereby the power of love is greater than the power of self-will. Rooted in the power of love, obedience becomes an expression of poverty, letting go of what we have made our own, our wills, and entrusting ourselves

into the hands of another. Obedience does not demand so much to do the will of another but rather to give oneself to another out of love. To be obedient therefore means truly listening to the other, respecting and desiring the best for the other.... Without obedience we become isolated and privatized individuals, locked up and enclosed within ourselves and cut off from the lifeline of God's love in the ordinary human person our neighbor, sister, brother, husband, child—and the simple ordinary goodness of everyday creation.

—Ilia Delio, *Clare of Assisi*

APPLICATION TO DAILY LIFE

- What authority do you have most difficulty obeying?
- What is the prudent way to make suggestions to those in authority?
- Can you think of a synonym for obedience?
- Try this week to make one positive suggestion to someone in authority—in your family, the Church, the state, your workplace.

PRAYER

I need a gentler spirit, Lord,
if I find myself wrestling with what the Church teaches.
Keep me mindful that this is your Church.
You are its head. You will keep it in your care.
Make me an obedient follower.
Amen.

PART THREE

....

Prayer

Prayer is the God-given means by which we move on our spiritual journeys of life. We may commit the entire Bible to memory. We may read ponderous volumes about Francis, Clare, other saints, and Church history. We may do good works that bring joy to the world. But, if we do not pray, we miss the intimate relationship with God that we are promised. Jesus said, "I am the way, and the truth, and the life. No one comes to the Father except through me" (John 14:6). We go to God through Jesus, through prayer. The following reflections may help you deepen and expand your prayer life. Wherever you are in your prayer life is a good beginning. Now Jesus challenges you to desire more from prayer. Be prepared to give and to receive more, much more.

....

The Spirit and Practice of Prayer

"St. Francis became a living prayer."
—Thomas of Celano, *The Life of St. Francis*

People who fall out of love—presuming they really were in love in the first place—are those who neglect to cultivate real intimacy. Husbands and wives may be very busy doing things that presumably express love—fixing up a home, getting kids to school or music lessons or soccer practice, repairing, saving, hurrying from task to task—but, if they do not stop in their hurried lives to simply sit down with each other in quiet but real communion of feelings, they are on a dead-end road.

So it is with our relationship with the God we cannot see. We can be very busy serving God, but if we do not work at a simple intimacy on a regular basis, we will also end up in a real or equivalent divorce from God.

We would like to say in our own defense, "But my whole life is a prayer! Why worry about some particular part of it?" That's an attractive temptation. It can gain support from Francis's famous phrase, "the spirit of prayer and devotion, to which all temporal things must be subservient." But the analogy of marriage is still true; wives and husbands wear themselves out doing all sorts of busy things for each other and the family. But if this supposedly healthy exterior is not nourished regularly by personal communion, it may become a substitute—or a flight from—real love.

Prayer is praying and nothing else. Prayer is not offering up our dish-washing, grass-cutting, snow-shoveling, and tire-changing. Prayer is looking at God, listening to God, responding to God and to nothing else. This means that there must be portions of our day when there is prayer and nothing else.

Prayer is the response of the human person to the personal approach of God. It doesn't treat God like some far-off potentate to whom we dutifully pay taxes in return for the benefits of citizenship. Prayer believes—perhaps with difficulty—that God wants a personal relationship with me that is unique, totally different from all the other relationships he has. My relationship with God depends on how I manage my relationships with others. But at the heart of my life is the call to personal intimacy with God. I achieve that purpose by receiving God—not mechanically, but consciously, willingly, reverently, and joyfully.

What, then, is prayer? It is two things. Prayer is our uniquely personal response to God's constant offer of himself. Prayer is a response that is separated from the rest of our lives in order that it may be the soul of the rest of our lives. Prayer is praying and nothing else. Prayer is direct communion with God.

Once this is established, we have almost an infinite number of choices as to the details. This is not saying that all roads then lead to the center, but it's saying that once the center is taken care of, all roads from the center lead to God.

The first word in prayer can be "I," but a more polite beginning is "you." The focus is placed on God. Francis gives us a perfect example of this in his Praises of God.

> You are the holy Lord God Who does wonderful things.
> You are strong. You are great. You are the most high.
> ...
> You are love, charity; You are wisdom, you are humility,
> ...
> You are beauty, You are meekness....
> Our happiness consists in praising the glory and goodness
> of God: We give you thanks for your great glory.

The second word may be "I." "I admit my sin, my weakness. I believe in your mercy. I open myself to your healing. I trust you. I am convinced that your presence and strength within me is the source of all holiness. I ask you confidently for all I need: for the health and welfare of my friends and enemies, for peace and justice, for your Church, for the salvation of the world."

QUESTIONS FOR REFLECTION

• What is essential to any personal relationship?
• What is prayer?
• How has your prayer changed over the years?

CONNECTING WITH SCRIPTURE

And whenever you pray, do not be like the hypocrites; for they love to stand and pray in the synagogues and at the street corners, so that they may be seen by others. Truly I tell you, they have received their reward. But whenever you pray, go into your room and shut the door and pray to your Father who is in secret; and your Father who sees in secret will reward you.

When you are praying, do not heap up empty phrases as the Gentiles do; for they think that they will be heard because of their many words. Do not be like them, for your Father knows what you need before you ask him.

Pray then in this way:
Our Father in heaven,
  hallowed be your name.
  Your kingdom come.
  Your will be done,
    on earth as it is in heaven.
Give us this day our daily bread.
And forgive us our debts,
  as we also have forgiven our debtors.

And do not bring us to the time of trial,
 but rescue us from the evil one.

For if you forgive others their trespasses, your heavenly Father
will also forgive you; but if you do not forgive others, neither will
your Father forgive your trespasses.

—Matthew 6:5–15

CONNECTING WITH FRANCISCAN WRITINGS

In the mountains everything was simpler and he confronted his
own aloneness there as he thought all must do from time to time.
But to wallow in a morbid concentration on himself was never his
inclination, and even alone on the mountain, he thought more of
Christ than of himself.

With Jesus, especially, Francis's kinship had ever been profound
and constant. He would stand at the foot of Mount Subasio and
wave, as if Jesus, alone in his cave at the top, were standing there
at the entrance waiting for him, eager to hear where he had been
and what had happened since the last time they shared the cave
together. He would run to the top and leap into the cave and
throw himself down on the cold stone where Jesus had lain in
wait for his return. The starkness of it all, the poverty, the rugged
toughness of life there at the top, thrilled him through to the
marrow of his soul.

It was then that he felt closest to them; for that void, that
emptiness, was the prelude to being filled with the Mountain
Man, with Christ Himself. At that point they were finally free of
Francis and ready to meet Jesus. They were then open, receptive,
emptied of all illusion and pretty daydreaming. They would, if
they reached that point and were strong enough to persevere, be
freed of loneliness and dependence forever.

—Murray Bodo, *Francis: The Journey and the Dream*

APPLICATION TO DAILY LIFE

- How does God enter into our prayer?
- If you are not already doing so, set aside this week a definite time for prayer in your day, perhaps as soon as you get up, or whatever time is best for quiet.

PRAYER

O God,
Help me to remember and to live St. Francis's words,
that if I am upset for any reason whatever,
I should immediately rise up to prayer
and remain in the presence of the Most High Father
for as long as it takes you to restore me to the joy of my salvation.
Amen.

Praying with God's Word

"Whenever I find his most holy name or writings
containing his words in an improper place, I make
a point of picking them up, and I ask that they be
picked up and put aside in a suitable place. We
should honor and venerate theologians, too, and
the ministers of God's word, because it is they
who give us spirit and life."

—St. Francis of Assisi, *The Testament*

The presence of Jesus is not limited to the appearances of
bread and wine. With God and the Holy Spirit, he is present
everywhere. God speaks to us by many means—the voices and
examples of others, our own experience of grace and sin, the
beauty and mystery of nature, but in a particular way, God speaks
to us in his inspired Word, the Scriptures. We may be sure of a
particularly powerful presence whenever we take up his words
with reverence.

Bible study is not prayer but preparation for prayer. However,
some acquaintance with the background of the various books of
the Bible is essential to a fruitful use of it in prayer.

When you use the Bible to pray, you are preparing to listen
to God with an open mind and heart. You believe God is now
speaking to you personally.

Read calmly, slowly, prayerfully. Have a plan, but do not try
to make so many yards a day. For instance, you may be praying
the Gospel of St. Matthew. Studying the book may take you six
months. Praying it may take you six years—or a lifetime. Simply
take a verse or two, or as many as you need, and listen to what

God is saying to you in your circumstances today. What is God calling you to be or to do? What acts of God are being illuminated? What reality in your own life—good or bad—is God pointing out? What motivation is being instilled in you?

This method of praying Scripture is sometimes called *lectio divina*. It consists of four steps and while seemingly simple, the process does take time.

> **Read.** Read a passage of Scripture slowly, thoughtfully, perhaps aloud.
>
> **Reflect.** Ask what the Scripture has to say to you at this particular time in your life. What is God saying to you through the Scripture?
>
> **Respond.** How does the Scripture make you feel? Are you willing to act as God seems to be directing you, or do you sense your own resistance? Talk to God about your response.
>
> **Receive.** Sit back quietly with the Scriptures and the message they have brought and be prepared to receive what God has for you. The insights, the inspirations, the challenges that come to you are God's gift. Receive that gift with a grateful heart.

Everyone will express their relationship in their own unique words and silences, looks, gestures, postures, actions, beings. Each of us responds according to our own personal makeup. Some are more emotionally enthusiastic than others. Some pray longer than others. Some are imaginative. Others are more formal. But in every case, real prayer means facing the reality of God with a pure heart and mind and giving the human response that truth lighted by the Spirit demands.

Francis was a man whom God led to almost an ecstatic reverence for the Word of God. The Bible was the source of his original inspiration. His first Rule was a collection of Bible texts. When he could not attend daily Mass, he had the Gospel of the day read to him from the missal. He said, "If I cannot be present at Mass, I adore the Body of Christ in meditation and with the eyes of the soul, in like manner as if I were present at Mass."

QUESTIONS FOR REFLECTION

- How can the Scriptures be used for prayer?
- What is the difference between studying the Bible and *lectio divina*?

CONNECTING WITH SCRIPTURE

The seed is the word of God. The ones on the path are those who have heard; then the devil comes and takes away the word from their hearts, so that they may not believe and be saved. The ones on the rock are those who, when they hear the word, receive it with joy. But these have no root; they believe only for a while and in a time of testing fall away. As for what fell among the thorns, these are the ones who hear; but as they go on their way, they are choked by the cares and riches and pleasures of life, and their fruit does not mature. But as for that in the good soil, these are the ones who, when they hear the word, hold it fast in an honest and good heart, and bear fruit with patient endurance.

—Luke 8:11–15

CONNECTING WITH FRANCISCAN WRITINGS

If you abide in me, and if my words abide in you, ask whatever you will and it shall be done to you (Jn 15:7). For where two or three are gathered together for my sake, there am I in the midst of them. (Mt 18:20). Behold I am with you even unto the consummation of the world (Mt 28:20). The words that I have spoken to you are spirit and life (Jn 6:64). I am the way, and the truth, and the life (Jn 14:6). And so we must hold fast to the words, the life, the teaching, and the holy Gospel of our Lord Jesus Christ. Of his own goodness, he prayed to his Father for us and made his name known to us, as he said: Father, I have manifested thy name to the men whom thou hast given me; because the words that thou hast given me, I have given to them. And they have received them, and have known of a truth that I came forth from thee, and they have believed that thou didst send me. I pray for them; not for the world do I pray, but for those whom thou hast given me, because they are thine, and all things that are mine are thine.

—St. Francis, *The Rule of 1221*

APPLICATION TO DAILY LIFE

- Reflect on a situation in your life that calls for decision-making. As you pray the Scriptures, ask God for wisdom in reaching a wise decision for that situation.
- Select a brief passage from Scripture and pray that Scripture each day, noting the insights that develop from your prayer.

PRAYER

I will rejoice in you, Lord, always.
I will rejoice because I know your kindness
and want to share it with others.
You are near.
I will not worry but in everything
through prayer with thanksgiving,
I will make my needs known to you.
I claim your peace, O God,
the peace that passes all human understanding
because you guard my heart and mind.
In Jesus's name.
Amen.

— adapted from Philippians 4:4–7

A Method of Praying

"Most High, Glorious God,
Enlighten the darkness of my heart.
Give me right faith, sure hope, and perfect charity.
Lord, give me insight and wisdom
So I might always discern
Your holy and true will."

—St. Francis of Assisi, "Prayer before the
Crucifix"

Meditation should not become an intellectual exercise or a complicated process that supposedly produces a grace-filled result. Meditation is best done by those who are childlike, sincere, and humble.

Meditation is simply the prayer that originates in our minds and hearts as compared with set prayers that others have given us. Meditation is informal, even though it may follow a general plan. Meditation is like the conversation of a child with a father or mother: perfectly open, trusting, simple, and filled with a great desire to please God.

This kind of prayer involves a bit of knowledge that it may be well done:

1. Create favorable circumstances. Select a period of time—ten, fifteen minutes, a half hour, an hour—when you will not ordinarily be disturbed. For many people this means early in the morning before the day begins to bustle. Be faithful to the time, no matter how you feel or what activities may threaten this time. It has been said that God redeems the time committed in prayer.

2. Ask the Holy Spirit to help you to be open to his light and warmth. Believe in the loving presence of this gift of God through Jesus and expect the grace of God to heal and recreate you. Sit expectantly in that presence.

3. Slowly read a passage of Scripture. You're not trying to get through a chapter. Perhaps one verse is enough. Place yourself within the scene in your imagination, if possible. Think of Jesus saying the words to you, doing these things for you. Note especially his feelings, how he sees and responds to God's will through his attitudes and reactions to the situation. As you read, stop, perhaps soon, perhaps only after a time, and talk to our Lord about what you have read—what he is saying to you personally. Prayer is your response to the Lord. You experience truth; you hear Christ speaking to you in it. You respond. That is prayer.

4. Some people are helped by writing their thoughts and responses on paper. You may want to keep your thoughts in a notebook or journal that's for you alone.

Gradually, Christ becomes more vivid to us. By trying to live like him, we learn to love him more. Certain aspects of his person begin to answer our deepest desires. We are not merely discovering the beauty of a truth; we are learning to love a person. Christ becomes someone living and present. I am not simply following him. The more detailed the comparison between Christ's life and mine, the more I can say, "I live, now not I, but Christ lives in me." That's what Francis did. That's what we are called to do.

Perhaps it is good to emphasize again that your response is your prayer. How will you respond? It depends on circumstances. You may feel love, hatred, joy, or sorrow. Desire, anger, fear or hope, shame, determination, trust, or humility may flood you. We react in many ways to God's truth.

Your response may be delight, admiration, adoration, or thanksgiving, or it may be begging, apology, peace, or generosity. Whatever your response, let it go wholeheartedly and honestly to Christ, your brother. If you have only one of these feelings or attitudes for half an hour, it doesn't matter. Just be yourself; be a child; trust God.

Above all, remember this. Your prayer really does not depend on how successful you are. You may feel miserable. God may seem to be a million miles away. God will accept your prayer not on the basis of how you feel but because you've reached out in prayer.

5. Finally, you'll want to end your prayer time properly. Conclude with, "Thank you, God, for helping me to pray." Then make a resolution, just one, to help you love God more. Keep doing these things, and your prayer will be an offering pleasing to God. And your life will become quite different!

QUESTIONS FOR REFLECTION

- What is the difference between prayer and meditation?
- Is there anything about meditation that makes you uncomfortable?

CONNECTING WITH SCRIPTURE

So I say to you, Ask, and it will be given to you; search, and you will find; knock, and the door will be opened for you. For everyone who asks receives, and everyone who searches finds, and for everyone who knocks, the door will be opened. Is there anyone among you who, if your child asks for a fish, will give a snake instead of a fish? Or if the child asks for an egg, will give a scorpion? If you then, who are evil, know how to give good gifts to your children, how much more will the heavenly Father give the Holy Spirit to those who ask him!

—Luke 11:9–13

CONNECTING WITH FRANCISCAN WRITINGS

The very first phrase in the Franciscan Rule reads, "The Rule and life of the Friars Minor is this, namely, to observe the Holy Gospel of our Lord Jesus Christ." Discover Christ in the Gospels and all of Scripture and in a prayerful way get deeper and deeper into his mind and heart, and then you can, as Francis liked to say, "follow the footprints of our Lord Jesus Christ." That is what Francis himself wanted to do and wanted his followers to do as well. He was not satisfied simply with knowing what Scripture said or being in awe of the wonderful God that he found there, but he had to give his whole self to follow Christ and through that give his whole self to God.

—Hilarion Kistner, *The Gospels According to Saint Francis*

APPLICATION TO DAILY LIFE

- What recurring situations in your life need more prayerful consideration?
- Be deliberate about opening your Bible and seeking for passages that will speak to you this week.

PRAYER

Lord, I often pray with many words.
Now I offer you my prayer of listening silence
in your holy presence...
Amen.

Christ Joins Us to His Prayer: The Liturgy

> "And the Lord gave me such faith in churches
> that I would pray with simplicity in this way and
> say: 'We adore You, Lord Jesus Christ, in all Your
> churches throughout the whole world, and we
> bless You because by Your holy cross You have
> redeemed the world.'"
>
> —St. Francis of Assisi, *The Testament*

Christ is always present in the Church but especially in her liturgical celebrations.

The mystery of Christ is that he reveals the mercy of God in human nature and saves us by his loving life, death, and Resurrection. The real nature of the Church is that it is consciously, freely, responsibly joined to Christ in his work. The Church is the sign or sacrament of Christ in the world today. We can no longer see him, yet we must continue to see him. He is visible in a body of people joined together, not merely by being physically next to each other in a building, but united in his grace, consciously feeling and exercising their responsibility to each other and to the world.

The Mass then is many things. The celebration of the Eucharist makes present the saving sacrifice of Christ. In it Christ joins his people into one worshiping body. It is the body of Christ— individuals freely joining others—accepting the salvation of Christ. The Mass is Christ worshiping, the Church worshiping with him.

Church is not some far-off abstraction—over there somewhere. Church is all of us, who by the grace of God voluntarily accept the call of Christ to be saved through him as members of his body. We are the Church!

This is not merely a functional arrangement. It is the very nature of things: I cannot love God without loving my neighbor and vice versa. I cannot love God as a human being without expressing this love through my body, visibly, externally. So the Mass, and all liturgy, expresses both my union with God and with my neighbor. Church is, therefore, a community or social matter and also a visible, external, public matter. Its purpose is to indicate that all that we do as Christians is ultimately directed to the praise of God with Christ our brother.

QUESTIONS FOR REFLECTION

- What is the real nature of the Church?
- Why must worship be communal and public as well as private?

CONNECTING WITH SCRIPTURE

When the hour came, he took his place at the table, and the apostles with him. He said to them, "I have eagerly desired to eat this Passover with you before I suffer; for I tell you, I will not eat it until it is fulfilled in the kingdom of God." Then he took a cup, and after giving thanks he said, "Take this and divide it among yourselves; for I tell you that from now on I will not drink of the fruit of the vine until the kingdom of God comes." Then he took a loaf of bread, and when he had given thanks, he broke it and gave it to them, saying, "This is my body, which is given for you. Do this in remembrance of me." And he did the same with the cup after supper, saying, "This cup that is poured out for you is the new covenant in my blood."

—Luke 22:14–20

CONNECTING WITH FRANCISCAN WRITINGS

Jesus in the sacrament dwelled in every church the brothers served, but no one would come to those churches unless the brothers there were holy. For Jesus manifests Himself in people, not in churches. Their faith and their love make the Sacrament real for those without faith. Bread and wine are transformed into Christ, and Christ eaten transforms people. And it is they, transformed, who touch others. Bread and wine remain just that to human eyes, but the people of God are somehow other than they were before the coming-in of Jesus.

Oh, the brothers! How long would they continue breathing in and breathing out the Lord? They were the Eucharist for those who could not fathom bread and wine as Christ. Would that every brother realized his witness to his fellows. The Eucharist meant nothing if those who ate it did not turn around and walk like children once again. The Eucharist was given for us, not we for Eucharist.

Oh, the brothers! Could they continue on the Journey nourished by their Lord alone? If they could not, then again the Eucharist would fail to be for them what Christ intended it to be. It was the Dream realized within them, it was food to make the Journey possible.

And when he thought now of the brothers, it was not just of the company of Lesser Brothers, but of all men and women of every time and place who breathed the Lord in and out as regularly as air. He thought of all who would let Christ transform them into what they needed to become in order to be happy. He found them in his own time and place, and he saw that transformation in their eyes. He saw them in the future, for the Word would always speak, and there would continue to be hearers of that Word. They would make the Eucharist convincing by the total transformation of their lives.

—Murray Bodo, *Francis: The Journey and the Dream*

APPLICATION TO DAILY LIFE

- Are you ready to accept the call to full, active, and conscious participation in the liturgy? Do you feel it is your right and duty to participate?
- Each time you share in the celebration of the Mass, try to consciously realize the various ways of participating: acclamations, responses, psalmody, antiphons, songs, actions, gestures, bodily attitudes, reverent silence.

PRAYER

O, God,
I praise and thank you
for being our God of celebration
who gathers us as a people in your name.
I long to experience you in worship
and in my fellow Christians.
Thank you for the privilege
of being one among many who love you.
Amen.

....

Eucharist: Contemplating the Mystery

"As He revealed Himself to the holy apostles in true flesh, so He reveals Himself to us now in sacred bread. And as they saw only His flesh by an insight of their flesh, yet believed that He was God as they contemplated Him with their spiritual eyes, let us, as we see bread and wine with our bodily eyes, see and firmly believe that they are His most holy Body and Blood living and true."

—St. Francis of Assisi, "Admonition I"

Because the Eucharist is a mystery, that is, it reveals as well as conceals God, we will never penetrate the full depth of its beauty. Christ gave us this mystery so that he could perpetuate the sacrifice of the Cross throughout the centuries until he comes again. In the words of the liturgy itself: "O holy banquet, in which Christ is received, the memory of his Passion is renewed, our spirit is filled with grace, and a pledge of future glory is given us."

The Mass is over in a relatively short time. We can scarcely become aware of even one of the great meanings before us, still less all of them. The following considerations are offered for meditation, for preparation and thanksgiving after Mass. Perhaps two a day this week will be most helpful to you. (They are taken from *Christian Commitment* by Father Karl Rahner.)

What we do at Mass:

• We utter with Christ his high priestly thanksgiving for creation and redemption. We have received, each in our own way, a share in the priesthood of Christ and we are able to stand before God and speak the thanksgiving of the whole world for his love and mercy.

- We enter freely into our Lord's own love made present to unite us. We accept it. We experience it for others. This is not a self-manufactured love we offer. We share it in the love that Jesus has for his Father. The Eucharist makes this visibly present to us so that we may enter into it.

- We celebrate the death of the Lord. To celebrate is to perform, do. We are made present to the life-giving death and resurrection of Jesus.

- We surrender ourselves to the weakness and vulnerability of man, our present subjection to death and evil, as the circumstances in which God's power works in us. We cannot save ourselves from the tragedy of sin that has blighted the whole human race. We accept ourselves as a sinful race called to the redemption that only God can achieve.

- We give our personal consent to the obedience with which Jesus died for us. We are not saved automatically even if the whole power of our salvation comes from Christ. We must pray for the gift to say "Yes!" freely, gladly, wholeheartedly.

- We renew our Lord's consent to the cross and death as the law of our own life. To live is to die to all that is not God, to die to all selfishness and self-sufficiency. To live is to be conscious and free with the power of the Spirit.

- We enter into the forgiveness of sins won by Christ's saving death and Resurrection. We accept forgiveness and offer it to others. The Eucharist is forgiveness. It is the sign of God's lifting us up from death and breathing his Spirit into us.

- We enter into the victory of Christ in his resurrection and glorification. We are already participants. Our life is a tension between the already—we already are in Christ, marked for resurrection—and the not yet—the full sharing in victory.

- We celebrate the resurrection and glorification of the Lord. It was not just his death that saved us. Inseparable from the cross, like the other side of the same coin, Jesus's glorious resurrection is the Father's promise to us also.

- We say "yes" to the new covenant sealed by the Blood of Christ. God has entered into a solemn pact with us as the Body of Christ. He is our God and we are his people.

- We enter into the coming of the Kingdom. The Kingdom is God possessing us in love. It is our freely opening ourselves to God's love. The Kingdom comes through Christ. It becomes visible through the Church, the sign lifted up among the nations.

- We ratify the transformation and forgiveness of the world which began with Christ's death and Resurrection. We are not passive spectators of salvation. We enter into the plan that lived in the heart of God from eternity.

- We look forward with confidence, hope, expectation to the coming of Christ. Judgment should be something we welcome, a declaration that we have accepted Christ and live his life. We have perhaps a natural fear of death, but we are also confident and eager to see Christ. Come, Lord Jesus!

- We receive the Body and Blood of Christ as a sign of the grace we have received and the grace we shall receive. There is no more perfect sacrament or sign of the love of God than this: he gives us himself in actual bodily union. He gives his whole being—God and man, soul and body. God actually wants to be united to us.

As we meditate on these profound mysteries, we may be moved to say with Francis:

"O sublime lowliness, O low sublimity! That the Lord of the universe, God and the Son of God, should so humble himself as to hide under the tiny little form of bread for our welfare. Look, brothers, at the humility of God and pour out your hearts before him. Be humble yourselves so that you may be exalted by him."

QUESTIONS FOR REFLECTION

- How is the Mass a mystery?
- What is the first purpose of the Mass?

CONNECTING WITH SCRIPTURE

I ask not only on behalf of these, but also on behalf of those who will believe in me through their word, that they may all be one. As you, Father, are in me and I am in you, may they also be in us, so that the world may believe that you have sent me. The glory that you have given me I have given them, so that they may be one, as we are one, I in them and you in me, that they may become completely one, so that the world may know that you have sent me and have loved them even as you have loved me. Father, I desire that those also, whom you have given me, may be with me where I am, to see my glory, which you have given me because you loved me before the foundation of the world.

Righteous Father, the world does not know you, but I know you; and these know that you have sent me. I made your name known to them, and I will make it known, so that the love with which you have loved me may be in them, and I in them.

—John 17:20–26

CONNECTING WITH FRANCISCAN WRITINGS

I beg you to show the greatest possible reverence and honor for the most holy Body and Blood of our Lord Jesus Christ through whom all things, whether on the earth or in the heavens, have been brought to peace and reconciled with Almighty God (cf. Col 1:20). And I implore all my friars who are priests now or who will be priests in the future, all those who want to be priests of the Most

High, to be free from all earthly affection when they say Mass, and offer single-mindedly and with reverence the true sacrifice of the most holy Body and Blood of our Lord Jesus Christ, with a holy and pure intention, not for any earthly gain or through human respect or love for any human being, not serving to the eye as pleasers of men (Eph 6:6). With the help of God's grace, their whole intention should be fixed on him, with a will to please the most high Lord alone, because it is he alone who accomplishes this marvel in his own way. He told us, Do this in remembrance of me (Lk 22:19), and so the man who acts otherwise is a traitor like Judas, and he will be guilty of the body and blood of the Lord (1 Cor 11:27).

—St. Francis, "Letter to a General Chapter"

APPLICATION TO DAILY LIFE

- Which of the many aspects of the Mass is most meaningful to you?
- How is all of life, not just the few minutes of Mass, the Eucharist or a thanksgiving?
- Pray this week for a deeper understanding of the true meaning of the Mass. Then, allow what you experience at Mass to change your approach to daily living.

PRAYER

"My God and my all."

—St. Francis

REFLECTION (28)

The Liturgy of the Hours

"And so I beseech the Minister General, my superior, to see that the Rule is observed faithfully by all, and that the clerics say the Office devoutly, not concentrating on the melody of the chants, but being careful that their hearts are in harmony— so that their words may be in harmony with their hearts—and their hearts with God. Their aim should be to please God by purity of heart, not to soothe the ears of the congregation by their sweet singing."

—St. Francis of Assisi, "Letter to
a General Chapter"

The Liturgy of the Hours is another way the Church gives us to heed the words of Francis that we are to work in such a way that we don't extinguish the spirit of prayer and devotion in our lives.

In addition to the official form of the Liturgy of the Hours, Francis composed several other forms for his followers. These include the Little Office of the Blessed Virgin Mary, the Office of the Passion, and the Office of the Twelve Our Fathers. Other forms of liturgical prayer containing psalms, Scripture reading and prayers, and special prayer forms of the liturgical seasons such as the Way of the Cross, the rosary, or Franciscan rosary can also be used.

The Liturgy of the Hours is the prayer of the Church. It is not, therefore, private, even when said by one person. Like all liturgy, it is the prayer of Christ and his Body carried throughout the whole day.

copied volume, it's not surprising that each monk was not issued his own psalter. This arrangement worked, since monks seldom left their monasteries.

However, for a new and rapidly growing order, the Franciscans, this system became a problem. These traveling preachers needed a way to pray the liturgical Hours on the road—a way that did not require carrying a library of oversized volumes with them. There already was a small, hand-held book of Hours in use at the papal court, called the Breviarum Curiae, or breviary. (Note the Latin root that gives us the word abbreviate.) The Franciscans obtained permission to use this, substituting the Gallican (French) Psalter for the Roman one. As the friars wandered through Europe doing the Lord's work, their small, portable breviaries were noticed, and desired, by clergy and monks everywhere. Other major orders soon followed suit with breviaries of their own.

Various editions of the Liturgy of the Hours are available in Catholic bookstores. The prayers can also be found online in a variety of forms. You might want to experiment with several different formats and translations to find one that meets your needs and your style of prayer.

QUESTIONS FOR REFLECTION

- Who should celebrate the Liturgy of the Hours?
- Why is it called the Liturgy of the Hours?

CONNECTING WITH SCRIPTURE

Let no one deceive you with empty words, for because of these things the wrath of God comes on those who are disobedient. Therefore do not be associated with them. For once you were darkness, but now in the Lord you are light. Live as children of light—for the fruit of the light is found in all that is good and right and true. Try to find out what is pleasing to the Lord. Take no part in the unfruitful works of darkness, but instead expose them. For it is shameful even to mention what such people do secretly; but everything exposed by the light becomes visible, for everything that becomes visible is light. Therefore it says,

"Sleeper, awake!

Rise from the dead,

and Christ will shine on you."

Be careful then how you live, not as unwise people but as wise, making the most of the time, because the days are evil. So do not be foolish, but understand what the will of the Lord is. Do not get drunk with wine, for that is debauchery; but be filled with the Spirit, as you sing psalms and hymns and spiritual songs among yourselves, singing and making melody to the Lord in your hearts, giving thanks to God the Father at all times and for everything in the name of our Lord Jesus Christ.

—Ephesians 5:6–20

CONNECTING WITH FRANCISCAN WRITINGS

The Franciscan path of prayer leads to peace because it is a path of active love. It is opening the mind and heart to the grace of God, and allowing God's grace to touch the deepest core of one's being. The path to peace means undergoing conversion in the deepest core of one's self and finding one's true self in God. It is a path of relationship with God that is centered on the Word made flesh, the person of Jesus Christ. Christ not only reveals God to us but Christ is the union of divine and human where the fullest possibilities of human life are joined with the fullness of God.

—Ilia Delio, *Franciscan Prayer*

APPLICATION TO DAILY LIFE

- As you pray portions of the Liturgy of the Hours, make a special effort to realize your union with Christ and the whole Church.
- Visualize yourself, as you pray this week, as an integral part of the faithful praying throughout the world.

PRAYER

"Come, let us worship the Lord who calls us to be his people. Amen."

Praying as a Group

"Wherever we are,
in every place,
at every hour,
at every time of the day,
every day and continually,
let all of us truly and humbly believe,
hold in our heart and love,
honor, adore, serve,
praise and bless,
glorify and exalt,
magnify and give thanks
to the Most High and Supreme Eternal God."
—St. Francis of Assisi, *The Rule of 1221*

Midway between the great liturgical prayer of the Church and the private prayer of individuals stands the prayer of a group of persons who voluntarily come together to pray. This form of prayer is less structured, more spontaneous than the prayer of the Mass and other sacraments. Recall that Christ promised, "For where two or three are gathered in my name, I am there among them" (Matthew 18:20).

Many people are helped by a loose structure for praying together: (1) an opening hymn, (2) silence and recollection, (3) the reading of a psalm, (4) response to the psalm by silence or spontaneous prayer of praise and thanksgiving, (5) the Magnificat or some other hymn, (6) prayers of petition, extended as long as desired, and (7) a closing prayer of thanksgiving to God.

Others may prefer unstructured prayer with no particular psalms or other prayers chosen ahead of time. The group simply gathers in reverent silence and awaits the inspiration of the Spirit to guide their prayer.

Though prayers of petition are a part of common prayer, the emphasis should be on praise and thanksgiving to the Father in the Spirit of Jesus. Though it is a group prayer, members should pay primary attention not to each other but to the presence of Christ. God- or Christ-centeredness is the heart of the prayer.

Extended moments of silence are frequent. Usually the more mature a group is in prayer, the richer are the silences since all are sharing consciously in the presence of God, and the more comfortable those praying will be with the periods of silence.

Shared prayer has a great amount of spontaneity. Yet like anything else worthwhile, it takes preparation. The preparation is the personal prayer of each individual and a serious attempt to be open to the Lord at all times. It is best to avoid conversation when the group gathers. A time for sharing will come later, but the first step is to pay full attention to the presence of God, inviting the Spirit to enlighten and empower the group to praise and thank God. A quiet space to gather, perhaps a lighted candle, and an open Bible help to focus the group.

Shared prayer is not a time for public confession or complaints about the difficulties of life, implicit condemnation of others piously prayed for, or any other kind of personal ostentation. A moment does come during the prayer time to speak a prayer of petition for one's personal needs and a time of sharing faith experiences with others. This supports and builds the faith of all the individuals present.

Some individuals may find it difficult or impossible to pray out loud in their own words before others. The group should accept this and not pressure anyone to produce. One can pray silently as well as audibly. What is important is that all are praying together in praise of God.

QUESTIONS FOR REFLECTION

- What is the purpose of shared prayer? How does it relate to our praying at Mass and as individuals?

CONNECTING WITH SCRIPTURE

As God's chosen ones, holy and beloved, clothe yourselves with compassion, kindness, humility, meekness, and patience. Bear with one another and, if anyone has a complaint against another, forgive each other; just as the Lord has forgiven you, so you also must forgive. Above all, clothe yourselves with love, which binds everything together in perfect harmony. And let the peace of Christ rule in your hearts, to which indeed you were called in the one body. And be thankful. Let the word of Christ dwell in you richly; teach and admonish one another in all wisdom; and with gratitude in your hearts sing psalms, hymns, and spiritual songs to God. And whatever you do, in word or deed, do everything in the name of the Lord Jesus, giving thanks to God the Father through him.

—Colossians 3:12–17

CONNECTING WITH FRANCISCAN WRITINGS

The simplest way to describe Franciscan prayer is that it begins and ends with the Incarnation. It begins with encountering the God of overflowing love in the person of Jesus Christ and ends with embodying that love in one's own life, becoming a new Incarnation. This is what it means to live the gospel life—not simply doing what Jesus did but opening up oneself to God who descends and takes on human flesh anew in the life of the believer.

To live the gospel life is to proclaim by one's life the Good News of God among us and thus to make Jesus Christ live anew.

—Ilia Delio, *Franciscan Prayer*

APPLICATION TO DAILY LIFE

- If you belong to a prayer group, reflect on whether the structure suggested here matches your experience. If not, what changes might you make?
- Gather for prayer with several friends. How might each person's individual prayer enhance the experience of all?

PRAYER

I ask you, Jesus, for spiritual friends
with whom I can gather to be in your presence,
to praise you, to talk with you, to listen to you.
Enter into our hearts and into our prayers
to make us one in you
with assurance that we will never face life alone.
Amen.

REFLECTION (30)

Clare: Bright Light

> "She was the first flower in Francis' garden, and
> she shone like a radiant star, fragrant as a flower
> blossoming white and pure in springtime."
> —St. Bonaventure, *Major Life of St. Francis*

What does Clare teach us about following Jesus? She teaches
us to follow Francis, who followed Jesus so perfectly and
so literally in pursuit of poverty, desiring nothing more than the
Lord. Clare teaches us that we can be committed faithful followers
of Francis and of Jesus while doing it in our own unique way
in accord with our circumstances in life. Both Clare and Francis
sacrificed all attachment to material possessions in their search for
the Christian life they were called to follow. Francis's journey took
him to distant places in his world. He walked hundreds of miles
around the peninsula now called Italy. He ventured to the land
of the Sultan of Damietta. In contrast, Clare journeyed the short
distance from her father's home to the little Church of Saint Mary
of the Angels, which Francis dubbed the Portiuncula, or Little
Portion. There she was received by the brothers. After a brief stay
with Benedictine nuns, she was to spend the remainder of her life
in the convent of San Damiano, the little chapel where the Lord
had spoken to Francis from the crucifix saying, "Go and rebuild
my Church."

Clare was to have a permanent home. Francis had special
places he visited, but if he were alive today, we might say he
had no permanent mailing address. Francis met and preached to
unknown numbers of people—on the dusty roads, in city squares,

in churches and chapels around the countryside, in foreign tents. Clare spread God's love through prayer, which attracted followers to her Franciscan way of life. Her prayers brought healings. She wrote letters to those in foreign lands, encouraging them in their Franciscan journeys. But she stayed close to home at San Damiano. Two dramatically different lifestyles followed the same goal: loving God with all their heart and soul and mind and strength.

Few of us are called to give away everything we possess. In many cases, that might actually be an ungodly thing to do because we have responsibilities for others—spouses, children, aging parents—that God entrusts to us. God has given us special gifts to use for his purposes—as workers in the marketplace, friends in the community, healers of the brokenhearted, lovers of the downtrodden. We won't shed our clothes on our village square in exchange for a ragged tunic with rope belt as Francis did. We won't have our hair shorn as a sign of humility in imitation of Clare. But we can devote our lives to following Jesus in the way of Francis and Clare in ways adapted to the time in which we live. The challenge of Francis and Clare to us is to discover that way and to persevere on its path in our own times in our own ways.

Even the twelfth-century hill town of Assisi vibrated with enough noise of humans, animals, carts, and wagons to drown the voice of silence. Not only sounds but reminders that there is something we must be doing that distracts us when we seek God in prayer. Both Clare and Francis sought quiet spots where they could hear the Lord speak in their hearts. They knew God had much to say to them if only they could hear the message. Clare's quiet place was the monastery; Francis retreated to mountain caves.

Our world is undoubtedly much noisier than Assisi eight centuries ago. Distractions abound. Noise thunders. Silence is a precious commodity, one to treasure. God has much to say to us, as he did to Clare and Francis, if we can find the space and place to listen.

Clare's name means "light." She is the bright, shining one who reflected God's love into the world from a cloistered convent where she lived with her spiritual sisters, first known as the Order of Poor Ladies, later the Poor Clares. That light continues today to shine through the Poor Clares throughout the world as they pray for our world.

Clare is also referred to as the "little plant" of Francis. One can visualize a branch plucked from a plant and stuck in the soil to take root to become a plant of its own. So was Clare's spiritual being rooted in Francis. Both of them were the branches grown from the Lord who proclaimed, "I am the vine, you are the branches" (John 15:5).

Christ is the mirror of God. "Mirror of Perfection" is a term used to describe Francis. And Clare was indeed a mirror of Francis. She caught what he taught by his way of life and then sent it into the world through her sisters, her prayer, her writing, and the Order she established. You and I can become mirrors of Jesus, Francis, and Clare in our own ways, in our own times.

QUESTIONS FOR REFLECTION

- What is your reaction to Clare's decision to leave her family's home to follow Francis?
- What aspect of Clare's way of following Francis and Jesus do you think you might incorporate into your life? What would you have to sacrifice?

CONNECTING WITH SCRIPTURE

We declare to you what was from the beginning, what we have heard, what we have seen with our eyes, what we have looked at and touched with our hands, concerning the word of life—this life was revealed, and we have seen it and testify to it, and declare to you the eternal life that was with the Father and was revealed to us—we declare to you what we have seen and heard so that you also may have fellowship with us; and truly our fellowship is with the Father and with his Son Jesus Christ. We are writing these things so that our joy may be complete.

—1 John 1:1–4

CONNECTING WITH FRANCISCAN WRITINGS

Evangelical life is gospel life, a life centered on living the gospel, following the footsteps of Jesus Christ. It is not surprising that both Francis and Clare begin their rules by saying, "The form of life… is this: to observe the Holy Gospel of our Lord Jesus Christ." In this way they indicated that the evangelical life is centered neither on work nor ministry but on how we experience the presence of God through Christ. The foundation of evangelical life is the human person and the sharing among persons of the experience of Christ.

—Ilia Delio, *Clare of Assisi*

APPLICATION TO DAILY LIFE

- Find a quiet space to spend time each day with God alone. Perhaps a room at home, a corner in the library on your lunch hour, a chapel, an empty workroom, or a park bench can become your monastery for a time of contemplation.
- How might you mirror Clare in your home or workplace today?

PRAYER

Brother Jesus,
through your radiant Chiara
you have reminded me of my need
to anchor my soul in a place of prayer,
a place where we can come together to worship the Father.

Free me from my restless activity,
my slavery to the clock,
my habit of bobbing along on the open sea
when you have called me to be still.

—Gloria Hutchinson, *Six Ways to Pray from Six Great Saints*

....

PART FOUR

Going Out into the World

Jesus sent forth his apostles to carry his word and work throughout the world. If we choose to follow Jesus and to lead others to his truth, we become modern-day apostles. We have a mission to go out to the world and show through our words and deeds the message of the Gospel. Some ways we might do this include leading a Scripture study group, working for reverence for all life in your community, or living a truly Christian life at your place of work. As part of our commitment to live like Francis, we are called to go out of ourselves to bring Jesus's gifts of faith, hope, and love to life in tangible, practical ways.

REFLECTION (31)

Family Life: Holiness in Its Place

"Happy are those who endure in peace. By you,
Most High, they will be crowned."
—St. Francis of Assisi, "The Canticle
of the Creatures"

The life of God is not lived in a vacuum. We do not become Christians and then withdraw from relationships with others. Holiness is not something we find outside normal, everyday human activity. Any and all fruits of following Christ with Francis must show up primarily in those relationships which are fundamental: family life. Charity and prayer, penance, poverty, humility—all must have their first fruits in what we contribute to the atmosphere of our home.

Our conventional wisdom and traditions are taught and experienced in our families. Parents do not merely produce children; they set the tone. It is true that outside influences seem to be having a greater impact today than before the Internet made us all-knowing, and cars and planes made us the most mobile creatures in history. But nothing can destroy the basic family unit.

Equally obvious is the fact that there would be no big Church were it not for thousands of little churches where the Gospel takes root in the most intimate of personal relationships: husband-wife, parent-child, brother-sister, cousins, grandparents, and so on! They will succeed to the degree that they have given and forgiven, agonized and rejoiced in the little community from which they come.

When Christianity pervades a whole way of life, it gradually

140

transforms it. We can experience that first in our families. In Christian homes, husbands and wives find their vocation in being witnesses to one another and to their children of faith in Christ and love for him.

Emphasis on the family as the foundation of Church and state inevitably introduces a comparison of married and single people. Those leading a celibate life, and perhaps also living alone, have their own witness to give. They do not share the particular satisfactions and problems of married life—a sacrifice on one hand, an advantage on the other. They may be freer to engage in apostolic activities outside the home. Their witness of a charitable, joyful, and chaste life is rightly honored as an integral part of the Church's life and activity.

QUESTIONS FOR REFLECTION

- What is the greatest gift parents have to give their children?
- In your own words describe the importance of family life in today's society.

CONNECTING WITH SCRIPTURE

When they had finished everything required by the law of the Lord, they returned to Galilee, to their own town of Nazareth. The child grew and became strong, filled with wisdom; and the favor of God was upon him.

Now every year his parents went to Jerusalem for the festival of the Passover. And when he was twelve years old, they went up as usual for the festival. When the festival was ended and they started to return, the boy Jesus stayed behind in Jerusalem, but his parents did not know it. Assuming that he was in the group of travelers, they went a day's journey. Then they started to look for him among their relatives and friends. When they did not find him, they returned to Jerusalem to search for him. After three days they found him in the temple, sitting among the teachers, listening to them and asking them questions. And all who heard him were amazed at his understanding and his answers. When his parents saw him they were astonished; and his mother said to him, "Child, why have you treated us like this? Look, your father and I have been searching for you in great anxiety." He said to them, "Why were you searching for me? Did you not know that I must be in my Father's house?" But they did not understand what he said to them. Then he went down with them and came to Nazareth, and was obedient to them. His mother treasured all these things in her heart.

And Jesus increased in wisdom and in years, and in divine and human favor.

—Luke 2:39–52

CONNECTING WITH FRANCISCAN WRITINGS

Most of his life he had been on the road to somewhere or from somewhere, or he had watched others doing the same. The earliest image he had of his father was that of a traveler. He always seemed to be gone, away in Northern Italy, or in the Provence of Southern France. His mother was the stable one, and he and his father moved toward and away from her. This traveler in him gave to his whole life a sense of movement.

From his mother he received his softness, his warmth, his music, and his poetry, for these were all of the Provence. His father had met Lady Pica in the Provence on one of his many trips into France to buy tapestries and cloth. He brought her home to Assisi, where she remained all her life while Pietro continued his forays into France. From his father Francis took his love of adventure, his stubborn adherence to his convictions, his practicality, and his journeying, restless soul. His father moved in his mind on continuous caravan routes to and from Assisi. And he continued to move there long after Francis' separation from him. He was always meeting Pietro at crossroads in his mind, and they would be reconciled at some deserted fork in the road, and Pietro would say he understood what Francis had to do that day before the Bishop of Assisi.

Perhaps that was one reason Francis was so often on the road. Perhaps he secretly hoped that his imaginings would come true. And now in the confusion of his dying hours, he could not remember if the reconciliation really did take place or if that rendezvous was kept in his imagination alone. He wanted to rise from the ground of his hut at St. Mary of the Angels and take to the road again. Or was his father dead? Yes, he had died that day in front of Bishop Guido. Or was it later? It really didn't matter now. He soon would meet his Heavenly Father face to face and He would tell him of Pietro.

Somehow he thought that their reconciliation was at hand, that the crossroads he had dreamed of was not of this time and place. It was somewhere else outside of time where every tear is dried and every wound is healed. Yes, he knew it. He and Pietro were about to join their hands and hearts once more. He wanted to burst into song in thanksgiving to God for this last Dream about to be fulfilled. And when he pictured God in his mind, God's face was suddenly Pietro's.

—Murray Bodo, *Francis: The Journey and the Dream*

APPLICATION TO DAILY LIFE

* Whether you are married or single, pay attention to the influences within your home, always seeking to strengthen your witness in following Christ.
* Choose one new activity this week to help bring your family unit (no matter its constellation) closer to each other and to God.

PRAYER

Thank you, Lord,
for the blessings and the challenges of my family
who help me become the special person I am created to be.
Help me to forgive the hurts of family life
and to rejoice in its miracles of love.
Amen.

REFLECTION (32)

Charity: Loving All People

"Wherever the friars meet one another, they should show that they are members of one family. And they should not hesitate to make known their needs to one another. For as a mother loves and cares for the child of her flesh, how much more should a friar love and care for his spiritual brother."

—St. Francis of Assisi, *The Rule of 1223*

To be God is to love. To share God's life, then, is to love like God, and indeed, to love like God made man. The essence of our faith is to love God and neighbor and self as Christ did and by the power of his Spirit. No one knew this better than Francis. His ideal was not merely to practice poverty, but to love the poor Christ and to be freed by the spirit of poverty from anything that might spoil his love of God and other people.

We cannot love others genuinely if we do not love ourselves. Many people are under the terrible handicap of thinking themselves to be worthless. They have such a low opinion of themselves that they cannot believe that others really love them. And because they think that they are practically worthless, they do not feel that they have anything to give to others.

Most of us are fortunate enough to have good mothers and fathers who gave us the conviction that we were important people. In the long process of maturing, we became whole by realizing that we are called to care for others just as our parents cared for us. Life is intended to be an ongoing process of creation whereby we all continue for each other what our parents started.

We are called to be cocreators with God of ourselves and of each other. Sometimes loving another person into wholeness is a difficult process of healing when one has not had the experience of being created by others' love.

Love is complex. It is learned gradually and grows in ongoing personal relationships. Gradually we come to learn that this wonderful experience we receive from others and return in kind is an earthly sharing of God's own life. We learn that all real love has its power from God and is divine (never merely "natural") whether we realize it or not. We learn that God loved the world so much that he made his love visible in Jesus and showed us the absolute height of love in the voluntary death of Jesus on the cross.

The love of Jesus for himself, for all people, and for God is the model and source of our own love. We really cannot love ourselves without realizing it is normal to go out of ourselves to love others. We cannot love others in a genuine way without being aware of God's presence in our love for each other. We cannot love God without wanting to share that relationship with others nor without realizing our own dignity.

Wherever there is genuine love, there is God. All real love is God's love. What, then, is distinctive about Christian love? It is a love that is conscious of the full extent of God's love made visible in Christ. Christian love is aware of all that God has said and done. It acts with the realization that the "love of God has been poured out in our hearts by the Holy Spirit, who is given to us." All that we do to others is done to Christ and for Christ. The only power to love that we possess is God's power in us. Christian love affirms that God has joined us together in his family, has made us a member of his divine community, and in Jesus has shown us a perfect model of love in the most difficult of circumstances.

Love is at the center of our lives because it is the highest manifestation of the life of God.

QUESTIONS FOR REFLECTION

• How would you describe true love?

• If love is real, is it supernatural?

CONNECTING WITH SCRIPTURE

If I speak in the tongues of mortals and of angels, but do not have love, I am a noisy gong or a clanging cymbal. And if I have prophetic powers, and understand all mysteries and all knowledge, and if I have all faith, so as to remove mountains, but do not have love, I am nothing. If I give away all my possessions, and if I hand over my body so that I may boast, but do not have love, I gain nothing.

Love is patient; love is kind; love is not envious or boastful or arrogant or rude. It does not insist on its own way; it is not irritable or resentful; it does not rejoice in wrongdoing, but rejoices in the truth. It bears all things, believes all things, hopes all things, endures all things.

Love never ends. But as for prophecies, they will come to an end; as for tongues, they will cease; as for knowledge, it will come to an end. For we know only in part, and we prophesy only in part; but when the complete comes, the partial will come to an end. When I was a child, I spoke like a child, I thought like a child, I reasoned like a child; when I became an adult, I put an end to childish ways. For now we see in a mirror, dimly, but then we will see face to face. Now I know only in part; then I will know fully, even as I have been fully known. And now faith, hope, and love abide, these three; and the greatest of these is love.

—1 Corinthians 13:1–13

CONNECTING WITH FRANCISCAN WRITINGS

Francis remembered the first victory of his new heart. All his life long he had panicked when he met a person with leprosy. And then one day on the road below Assisi, he did one of those surprising things that only the power of Jesus' Spirit could explain. He reached out and touched such a one, the very sight of whom nauseated him. He felt his knees playing tricks on him, and he was afraid he would not make it to the leper standing humbly before him. The odor of rotting flesh attacked his senses as if he were smelling with his eyes and ears as well. Tears began to slide down his cheeks because he thought he wouldn't be able to do it; and as he began to lose his composure, he had to literally leap at the man before him. Trembling, he threw his arms around the leper's neck and kissed his cheek.

Then, like the feeling he remembered when he first began to walk, he was happy and confident; he stood erect and calm and loved this man in his arms. He wanted to hold him tighter but that would only be to satisfy himself now; and he was afraid to lose this newfound freedom. He dropped his arms and smiled, and the man's eyes twinkled back their recognition that Francis had received more than he had given. In the silence of their gazing, neither man dropped his eyes, and Francis marveled that a leper's eyes were hypnotically beautiful.

—Murray Bodo, *Francis: The Journey and the Dream*

APPLICATION TO DAILY LIFE

- Why do you love God?
- Would you say that you love yourself?

PRAYER

Lord, I used to think charity meant giving away something, and it does mean that.

Thank you for enabling me to see that meaning in a new way: Charity means giving myself away in love to you and to others. Please keep me from being stingy in giving of myself. Amen.

REFLECTION (33)

The Forgiveness of Christ

"There should be no friar in the whole world
who has fallen into sin, no matter how far he has
fallen, who will ever fail to find your forgiveness
for the asking, if he will only look into your eyes.
And if he does not ask forgiveness, you should
ask him if he wants it. And should he appear
before you again a thousand times, you should
love him more than you love me, so that you may
draw him to God; you should always have pity
on such friars."

—St. Francis of Assisi, "Letter to a Minister"

The true test of our charity is the situation in which we are not
loved: Someone does not apologize; someone continues to do
something that irritates, exasperates, hurts, or injures us. In that
precise situation Christ says, "But I say to you, Love your enemies
and pray for those who persecute you" (Matthew 5:44).

It is very easy to like and love good people. It may be relatively
easy to forgive those who beg our pardon. We admire those who
forgive a dramatic injury. But the greatest test of our love of God
and neighbor comes in those thousand daily incidents in which
we do not get our way, those times when others inflict their will
on us.

Forgiveness is not incompatible with the just pursuit of our
rights. We may be forced to speak up when there is a question of
injustice to ourselves or others. We may have to call the police,
sue, go to a higher authority, argue, persist. But even in the midst

of these activities, the challenge of forgiveness is to love the other person in spite of the action.

God's love never changes. His love does not depend on our virtue (though our happiness does). God's forgiveness simply means that he keeps loving us as he always did. Since our God is that way and we have that divine life, we have no choice but to act the same way. We have the privilege of being like God. Note the reason Jesus gave for forgiving our enemies, "You may be children of your Father in heaven; for he makes his sun rise on the evil and on the good, and sends rain on the righteous and on the unrighteous" (Matthew 5:45). If being like God isn't enough reason to forgive, there is no reason good enough.

No matter what others have done to us, we can and must wish them the blessing of God. We do not have to go out of our way in displaying affection. But we must give this person the civilities that all good people would expect us to give even in these circumstances. Forgiveness does not mean liking what another does.

One of the beautiful incidents in St. Francis's life centered around forgiveness. Francis found a man bitterly cursing the employer who had cheated him—literally wishing that God would damn him. Francis begged him to find forgiveness in his heart so that the man could free himself. We cannot be free, peaceful children of God if we nourish a vindictive attitude in our heart.

QUESTIONS FOR REFLECTION

• What does it mean to forgive?
• Why should you forgive your neighbor?

CONNECTING WITH SCRIPTURE

Then Peter came and said to him, "Lord, if another member of the church sins against me, how often should I forgive? As many as seven times?" Jesus said to him, "Not seven times, but, I tell you, seventy-seven times.

"For this reason the kingdom of heaven may be compared to a king who wished to settle accounts with his slaves. When he began the reckoning, one who owed him ten thousand talents was brought to him; and, as he could not pay, his lord ordered him to be sold, together with his wife and children and all his possessions, and payment to be made. So the slave fell on his knees before him, saying, 'Have patience with me, and I will pay you everything.' And out of pity for him, the lord of that slave released him and forgave him the debt. But that same slave, as he went out, came upon one of his fellow-slaves who owed him a hundred denarii; and seizing him by the throat, he said, 'Pay what you owe.' Then his fellow-slave fell down and pleaded with him, 'Have patience with me, and I will pay you.' But he refused; then he went and threw him into prison until he should pay the debt. When his fellow-slaves saw what had happened, they were greatly distressed, and they went and reported to their lord all that had taken place. Then his lord summoned him and said to him, 'You wicked slave! I forgave you all that debt because you pleaded with me. Should you not have had mercy on your fellow-slave, as I had mercy on you?' And in anger his lord handed him over to be tortured until he should pay his entire debt. So my heavenly Father will also do to every one of you, if you do not forgive your brother or sister from your heart."

—Matthew 18:21–35

CONNECTING WITH FRANCISCAN WRITINGS

The key to Francis' transformation into love, his secret of making wholes out of the scattered fragments of life, was compassion. He learned compassion as the art of healing broken hearts by collecting the tears of the forgotten, the frightened, and the lonely in his hands and holding the wounded as his kin. Francis entered the world of the stranger and made the stranger into a brother. He learned to love what was weak and fragile, and he learned to care for what the world discarded.

—Ilia Delio, *Compassion*

APPLICATION TO DAILY LIFE

- How can you best go about forgiving the person who irritates you the most?
- As you pray the Our Father, think of the mercy available to you by forgiving others.

PRAYER

"Forgive us our trespasses
as we forgive those who trespass against us."
You did that, Jesus.
Help me to forgive as you did.
Amen.

Being Christ to Others

"In St. Francis' later life, a leper occasioned another beautiful example of his charity and its Christlike power. The leper complained that the Brothers did not take care of him properly. Francis simply said, 'Shall I take care of you?' The leper answered, 'I would like that.' Francis said, 'I will do all you wish.' The leper, 'Then I want you to wash me all over, the odor is so bad, I cannot stand it.' Then Francis took warm water and aromatic herbs, undressed the sick man and began to wash him. As he touched the leper's body with his hands, the leprosy began to be cured. And the man's soul began to be cured also. The leper began to cry, first softly, then aloud. 'I am worthy of hell for the injustice I have done the Brothers, and for my impatience and blasphemy.' But Francis thanked God for so great a miracle and hurried away, lest honor come to him."

—Johannes Jorgensen, *St. Francis of Assisi*

Almost everybody has asked the question, at least in his heart, "How can I possibly see Christ in him? In her?" Perhaps we will find the answer by first taking care of being Christ to others. We may then find him very easily in those we serve.

We, the body of Christ, continue the life and work of Christ on earth today. If the world is to know how Christ loves, heals, forgives, it must have visible examples in the members of the Church.

Now, the essence of the life of Christ is that he simply "went about doing good." He continues that activity today. The Head needs the hands, even ours, to bless and heal and wash the wounds of others.

We are called to speak to others, offering understanding, encouragement, cheerfulness, patience, peace. We can help them carry their burdens. We can remind them through our words—but even more through our actions—that God loves them. We are to be open to the needs of others, but also respect their privacy and dignity. This might mean supporting them in their physical, emotional, or spiritual suffering; it might be giving them food, clothing, and shelter. But it might also mean supporting them in their fight for human rights, for a decent opportunity to grow as human beings and children of God.

We have been made adopted children of the Father, possessing God's own life. The most obvious result is that we are to act like God, as every child acts like its father and mother. To be a Christian is to love as God loves or as Christ loves—which is the same thing. This is not merely imitating externally what Christ did on earth. We have an inner reality, the life of God living within our freedom, whereby we love as God loves, with his power, joy, and fruitfulness.

Francis had a great love for his mother's homeland, France, and for its tales of knightly glory and courtly love. After his conversion, the delicate courtesy and respect for every person remained. One night, when Francis and the brothers were staying at Rivotorto, a voice was heard in the crowded little dormitory. "Oh, I am dying, I am dying!" Francis and the other friars awakened and struck a light. Francis asked, "Who is dying?" One of the friars confessed that he was dying of hunger. Instead of dressing the man down as a weakling among giants in asceticism, Francis gently suggested that they all have a snack. For Francis, courtesy and hospitality, compassion for another's suffering, was more important than his own rules for fasting.

Being Christ is not only giving one's life on the cross. It is ordering food for a little girl just raised from the dead, asking for a drink of water because the Samaritan woman needed his healing, being concerned about the embarrassment of a bride and groom at Cana, and putting his arms around the little children.

QUESTIONS FOR REFLECTION
• How can you continue the charity of Christ?

CONNECTING WITH SCRIPTURE
And during supper Jesus, knowing that the Father had given all things into his hands, and that he had come from God and was going to God, got up from the table, took off his outer robe, and tied a towel around himself. Then he poured water into a basin and began to wash the disciples' feet and to wipe them with the towel that was tied around him.... After he had washed their feet, had put on his robe, and had returned to the table, he said to them, "Do you know what I have done to you? You call me Teacher and Lord—and you are right, for that is what I am. So if I, your Lord and Teacher, have washed your feet, you also ought to wash one another's feet. For I have set you an example, that you also should do as I have done to you."

—John 13:3–15

CONNECTING WITH FRANCISCAN WRITINGS
The society of Assisi was divided into the majores and the minores, and Francis had moved from the "greater ones" to the "lesser ones" when he finally met Jesus. He called his brotherhood the Fratres Minores, the Lesser Brothers, and he wanted them always

to be associated with the poor, the lesser people in society. That desire was a constant source of amazement to people, for all wanted to "better" their condition and become more wealthy and comfortable as they built solidly for the future. Money was the foundation of their faith, securing their castles against the storms of circumstances and fate. Francis and the brothers had battered against these frail foundations, and in the course of years, many in Umbria had come to see that the brothers were right.

At first the people scoffed at them and complained bitterly of these lazy bums who lived off the responsible, respectable citizenry. Sure, these brothers "gave up" everything all right. But the next day they were at your door begging for a share of what you worked so hard to provide for your family. They must think that Assisi is a tiered layer cake baked into the side of Mount Subasio that they can cut into anytime they like.

But later the example of the brothers won out, and the citizens considered them essential witnesses in their midst. To Francis, the most gratifying example of their change of heart came when he returned from the Holy Land and called the first major gathering of the brothers. Five thousand of them met at St. Mary of the Angels. For eight days, they lived in the open air or in little huts of woven boughs, and such a huge crowd was anything but a model spectacle of cleanliness and order. But despite the unkempt appearance of this motley crew of beggars, the citizens of Assisi now knew that they were real leaven. The brothers had been faithful to Lady Poverty and in return the townsfolk showered them with food and considered it a privilege to do so. How great the power of the Gospel Life when lived sincerely and unconditionally!

—Murray Bodo, *Francis: The Journey and the Dream*

APPLICATION TO DAILY LIFE

• How can you be Christ in your own home? On the street? At work?

• Ask yourself as often as possible: What would Christ do right now? What does Christ wish you to do—and to do in you— right now?

PRAYER

Lord Jesus,
it has been said that you have
no hands for your work and caring on earth today
except our hands.
Please use mine.
Amen.

REFLECTION (3 5)

Seeing Christ in Others

"Whoever comes to them, friend or foe, thief
or robber, let him be received with kindness....
They must rejoice when they live among people
considered of little value and looked down upon,
among the poor and the powerless, the sick and
the lepers, and the beggars by the wayside."

—St. Francis of Assisi, *The Rule of 1221*

True love is not divisible. Genuine love of God implies love
of neighbor and self. Genuine love of neighbor and self can
come only out of a love of God. Even in the most vindictive,
inconsiderate, domineering person, we are called to see God.
Beneath the sin and ugliness, everyone mirrors at least some of
the attributes of God: free, intelligent, capable of the highest love.
Even if that freedom has been enslaved or that intelligence is
clouded by physical, emotional, or moral obstacles, that person
is still full of potential.

Christ brought new dignity to human nature by the union of
the divine and the human. In the one person of Christ, human
nature is inseparably and forever united to God. Christ did not
add anything to human nature. Rather he made visible the love
that had never changed. The first human beings were already
loved with this love and the theology of Duns Scotus holds that
from eternity Christ was destined to be the head and center of the
human race simply because God is love.

Every human being is clothed in the love of God and marked
with the most perfect visible sign of God's love—a human nature

like that of Christ. We are the unfinished children of God. God is working hard on us. God has no difficulty in seeing the end-product he has in mind—unique human beings, each bearing a family likeness to the firstborn Son.

God's intention is that every person we meet be with us someday in heaven, purified and glorious, with intelligence balanced and brilliant, with love made Christlike and with a body radiant and perfect. We must see this now. For this will be our judgment: "I was hungry [for kindness] and you gave it. I was thirsty [for patience] and you gave it. I was sick [with sin] and you took care of me. I was in the prison [of my own selfishness] and you helped me break the chains."

QUESTIONS FOR REFLECTION
- Why does God love every human being?
- What is God's plan for everyone?

CONNECTING WITH SCRIPTURE
But I say to you that listen, Love your enemies, do good to those who hate you, bless those who curse you, pray for those who abuse you. If anyone strikes you on the cheek, offer the other also; and from anyone who takes away your coat do not withhold even your shirt. Give to everyone who begs from you; and if anyone takes away your goods, do not ask for them again. Do to others as you would have them do to you.

If you love those who love you, what credit is that to you? For even sinners love those who love them. If you do good to those who do good to you, what credit is that to you? For even sinners do the same. If you lend to those from whom you hope to receive, what credit is that to you? Even sinners lend to sinners, to receive as much again. But love your enemies, do good, and lend, expecting nothing in return. Your reward will be great, and you will be children of the Most High; for he is kind to the ungrateful and the wicked. Be merciful, just as your Father is merciful.

—Luke 6:27–36

CONNECTING WITH FRANCISCAN WRITINGS

He'd only been on the road a day or so when, in the city of Spoleto, he began again to hear voices in the night.

"Francis, is it better to serve the Lord or the servant?"

"Oh, sir, the Lord, of course."

"Then, why are you trying to turn your Lord into a servant?"

And Francis, trembling in recognition, replied, "Lord, what do You want me to do?"

"Go home, Francis, and think about your first vision. You have seen only the appearances and not the heart of glory and fame. You are trying to make your vision fit your own impatient desire for knighthood."

And Francis, shaken and fully awake, understood now that he had taken too much into his own hands. He realized that impatience had driven him to act too quickly and that he must wait and listen and purify his heart to hear deeper words than he had imagined. He had tried to make God's will serve his own impatient desire for glory. He had not really listened. The road back to Assisi seemed to shake beneath him. As a knightly figure returning home alone, he seemed to shout, "I am retreating," for the world to hear. But he didn't mind the quizzical looks and the scorn on the faces of the peasants who stared at him.

—Murray Bodo, *Francis: The Journey and the Dream*

APPLICATION TO DAILY LIFE

• What does God see of Christ in you?
• Why are you lovable?
• Make a deliberate effort to see Christ in one definite person.

PRAYER

Teach me, Lord, to look deeply into others to find you there.
It's so easy to focus on the unfinished part of a person
and miss your Spirit that might be veiled
behind a grumpy face, an angry word, a proud expression.
Give me the eyes of your Spirit to see as you see.
Amen.

....

Justice: The First Requirement of Charity

"Let no man therefore imagine that a life of activity in the world is incompatible with spiritual perfection. The two can very well be harmonized. It is a gross error to suppose that a man cannot perfect himself except by putting aside all temporal activity, on the plea that such activity will inevitably lead him to compromise his personal dignity as a human being and as a Christian..... Animated, too, by the charity of Christ, he finds it impossible not to love his fellow men. He makes his own their needs, their sufferings and their joys."

—Pope John XXIII, *Mater et Magistra*, 255, 257

We can make two serious errors about justice and charity. First, we can think that justice concerns what we must do for others and that charity is what we may do for them—a sort of bonus virtue. Second, we can put justice in the category of things—pay the money you owe—and charity in the area of persons—love your neighbor.

This unfortunate divorce has enabled us to be very honest—we couldn't think of stealing a dime—and yet quite unconcerned about the fact that many of our brothers and sisters live in a state of perpetual deprivation of the most basic rights. We may believe that it is charitable to send them donations of food and old clothing. But we didn't owe them anything in the way of structural or institutional change.

Justice is impossible without love. Love is absolute and irreplaceable. All other virtues and practices must be expressions of it. If justice is to be a Christian value, it must be a justice of love or it is no justice at all. There is an urgent need to be concerned about justice on a more basic level, particularly with a concern for the poor, the deprived, the unemployed, the uneducated, and the handicapped. The greatest injustice is perpetuated by institutions, the complex systems humans devise to fulfill their purposes. Injustice can be built into the very culture and social customs of a nation.

Discriminative housing patterns are supported by people who say they want only what is best for their children and who say they want to maintain quality education. Deceit in government is approved by all who claim that you have to cut a few corners to get someplace. Trade agreements keep developing that push countries into a state of poverty because we must keep our own economy healthy.

As Johannes Jorgensen noted in his *St. Francis of Assisi: A Biography*:

> Most people would not immediately think of St. Francis as a social reformer, yet the Third Order itself was a great instrument of reform. No lay Franciscan was allowed to bear arms to be used against any person. This was a deadly blow against a system of enforced military service whereby petty feudal lords could force their subjects into fighting their wars of conquest and revenge. At Faenza, for instance, many of the citizens had joined the Penitential Brothers, as the Third Order was then called. When the mayor wished them to take the usual oath of obedience whereby they would oblige themselves to take up arms when the authorities ordered it, they refused to swear (shades of our modern conscientious objectors!) under the

claim that to swear such an oath involved taking up arms, and that was against their Rule. The mayor tried to force the Brotherhood to take the oath. Apparently they turned in their need to Francis's friend, Cardinal Hugolino. The Pope then ordered the bishop to take the Penitential Brothers under his protection. This dispute soon spread all over Italy. As a sort of punishment, the cities subjected the Penitential Brothers to special taxes and forbade their giving their property to the poor. In a circular letter to all Italian bishops, the Pope ordered all the clergy to take the side of the Brothers against the public authorities. And so the Third Order brought about at least a partial disarming of the quarrelsome Italian republics.

Franciscans living in the world today may not have such a clear-cut choice as taking or rejecting a military oath. But the fact that our problems are complex and emotional is no excuse for avoiding them. Justice is a matter of taking charity seriously. If we are with the Church as Francis was, then we will be challenged by the clear call to action given by Pope Paul and the bishops at the 1971 Synod on Justice in the World: "Action on behalf of justice and participation in the transformation of the world fully appear to us as a constitutive dimension of the preaching of the Gospel." In other words, action for justice is one of the elements that constitutes the proclamation of the Good News. If it is missing, the Gospel is crippled.

QUESTIONS FOR REFLECTION

• What might justice without charity look like? Charity without justice?

CONNECTING WITH SCRIPTURE

I hate, I despise your festivals,
    and I take no delight in your solemn assemblies.

Even though you offer me your burnt-offerings and grain-offerings,
  I will not accept them;
  and the offerings of well-being of your fatted animals
  I will not look upon.
Take away from me the noise of your songs;
  I will not listen to the melody of your harps.
But let justice roll down like waters,
  and righteousness like an ever-flowing stream.

—Amos 5:21–24

CONNECTING WITH FRANCISCAN WRITINGS

As soon as he had heard the news of the wolf of Gubbio, Francis felt sympathy for the wolf. There was something of the wolf in all of nature, that ravenous hunger, that restless pursuit, that baring of the fangs, so symbolic of what was wild and violent in all of us. But he saw in the wolf not so much the stalker as the stalked. Everyone feared wolves and disliked them, and he saw in the eyes of wolves a fear, a hunted look, an anger and hostility that wanted to devour everything in sight in order to avenge their own hurt and alienation. Wolves, after all, were like people. If you feared them and ostracized them and excluded them, they eventually turned into what you were afraid they were anyway.

...

Francis and the woman were drawing close to the rock. Suddenly, without warning, they heard behind them a low growl and a pounding of the ground. Spinning around, Francis saw the wolf charging wildly toward them. Francis made the Sign of the Cross, first over the petrified woman and then over the wolf. He took a deep breath and started walking slowly toward him. The wolf slowed his pace and then came to an abrupt stop.

...

Francis spoke. "Brother Wolf, in the name of Jesus, our brother, I have come for you. We need you in the city. These people here have come with me to ask you, great ferocious one, to be the guardian and protector of Gubbio. In return we offer you respect and shelter for as long as you live. In pledge of this I offer you my hand." He stretched out his hand. The wolf seemed calm, but he remained immobile, scanning the crowd with his large, bloodshot eyes. Then slowly he walked to Francis and lifted his paw into his warm, steady hand. The two remained in that position for a long time and what they said to one another Francis never told to any living soul. Finally, Francis leaned over and put his arms about the wolf's neck. Then he and his new brother walked meekly up to the brave peasant woman and the three of them led the stunned, silent crowd back to Gubbio.

—Murray Bodo, *Francis: The Journey and the Dream*

APPLICATION TO DAILY LIFE

- What do you think is the greatest injustice in your state, county, city, or neighborhood? In your own way of looking at life?
- Try to examine your language and conversation for unrealized expressions of prejudice.

PRAYER

I ask you, Lord,
for a heart that loves enough
to want the best for all people.
Amen.

REFLECTION (3 7)

Justice: Bringing the Gospel to the World

"The faithful, and more precisely the laity, are stationed in the front ranks of the Church, and through them the Church is the living principle of human society. Consequently, they especially must have an ever clearer consciousness, not only of belonging to the Church, but of being the Church."

—Pope Pius XII, *Acta Apostolicae Sedis,* 38

The popes in their encyclicals tell us that we have a double duty. We must try to produce a morally better society, and we must try to produce a society whose institutions are better. The word *institution* simply means the big, organized ways by which society takes care of its needs and keeps the wheels of civilization moving ahead. Certain basic needs of humankind have always been present. They may have been taken care of in different ways, but the basic needs are the same:

Political: some kind of governing organizations.

Economic: some method of producing and distributing goods.

Educational: some method of training and teaching the young.

Family: a system of family life to continue the race.

Recreational: a general way of diversion and play.

Religious: a way to worship God as a community.

A few people will be in positions to influence society directly: those who hold important positions in government, business, unions, and community organizations. Most people can help only indirectly. Perhaps the greatest need today is education in the social teachings of the Church. Many a good movement dies because people are not interested. They are not interested because they do not know anything about these topics.

However, while the unity of a group endeavor may carry greater influence in reforming institutions, we must never forget that most group activities begin with the discernment of need, the vision and the energy of an individual. As individuals we must never feel we are powerless when we act for justice.

QUESTIONS FOR REFLECTION
- What is our double duty?
- What are the institutions of society? How might they need to be reformed in light of the Gospel?

CONNECTING WITH SCRIPTURE

Moses was keeping the flock of his father-in-law Jethro, the priest of Midian; he led his flock beyond the wilderness, and came to Horeb, the mountain of God. There the angel of the Lord appeared to him in a flame of fire out of a bush; he looked, and the bush was blazing, yet it was not consumed. Then Moses said, "I must turn aside and look at this great sight, and see why the bush is not burned up." When the Lord saw that he had turned aside to see, God called to him out of the bush, "Moses, Moses!" And he said, "Here I am." Then he said, "Come no closer! Remove the sandals from your feet, for the place on which you are standing is holy ground." He said further, "I am the God of your father, the God of Abraham, the God of Isaac, and the God of Jacob." And Moses hid his face, for he was afraid to look at God.

Then the Lord said, "I have observed the misery of my people who are in Egypt; I have heard their cry on account of their taskmasters. Indeed, I know their sufferings, and I have come down to deliver them from the Egyptians, and to bring them up out of that land to a good and broad land, a land flowing with milk and honey, to the country of the Canaanites, the Hittites, the Amorites, the Perizzites, the Hivites, and the Jebusites. The cry of the Israelites has now come to me; I have also seen how the Egyptians oppress them. So come, I will send you to Pharaoh to bring my people, the Israelites, out of Egypt." But Moses said to God, "Who am I that I should go to Pharaoh, and bring the Israelites out of Egypt?" He said, "I will be with you; and this shall be the sign for you that it is I who sent you: when you have brought the people out of Egypt, you shall worship God on this mountain."

—Exodus 3:1–12

CONNECTING WITH FRANCISCAN WRITINGS

"The kingdom of heaven suffers violence and only the violent bear it away." He had lived in an age of violence, an age when to die in battle was a glorious passing. In conformity with his times he, too, had twice ridden off to battle to prove himself a man. But with his conversion came the realization that war and violence mocked the Gospel of Jesus and that going to war proved nothing.

He had wanted to confront people with the peace of Jesus in a way that would be convincing. So he did it with something like violence. He did violence to himself and he did violence to his age by turning upside down what it believed in. He wanted to be a knight. So he became a beggar and acted like a knight. He wanted honor and fame. So he put on shame and anonymity. He wanted to conquer the world. So he let Christ conquer him.

The only violence he knew was the violent, unswerving adherence to the Dream. He would let no one destroy it with sweet words or strong words, with false meekness or power of persuasion. He had set about to win over the forces of evil with the same determination that he set out to win the battle against Perugia when he was a young man. He insisted, against all opposition, that the Gospel could be lived, or at least that one man could live it if he let Jesus take over his life.

He understood from the beginning, when he began repairing the church of San Damiano, that it takes a violent will to persevere in good and that violence wreaked on others is weakness and betrays despair. The violence of the good could turn aggression into virtue.

But the good were becoming weak and evil was growing as people did what was comfortable and safe to do, be it good or evil. He wanted the brothers—all people—to insist on love with the violence of those with a purpose. The Journey was a determined advance, not a leisurely stroll through the countryside. The Kingdom of Heaven had to be taken, not expected as a gift. True, it was a gift from God, but only if you set out to win it. Your will had to be turned irrevocably toward God before He gave you freely what you came to take by storm.

—Murray Bodo, *Francis: The Journey and the Dream*

APPLICATION TO DAILY LIFE

- Take one action this week toward justice in your community.
- Examine your conscience to discover whether you have been selfish in regard to your obligation to society.

PRAYER

Each of your saints, Lord,
possesses the quality of courage.
Fill me with your strength of heart,
called courage,
to live the Gospel in a world
that too often denies that you are Lord.
Amen.

Justice: Our Pressing Social Problems

*"Where there is hatred, let me sow love, where
there is injury, pardon."*
                    —Peace Prayer, attributed to St. Francis

P ope Paul VI issued an apostolic letter, "A Call to Action,"
on the eightieth anniversary of Pope Leo's great encyclical,
Rerum Novarum. Pope Paul spelled out new areas which Christian
social justice must consider. This chapter touches upon some of
the issues which most concerned him. Sadly, they are still largely
unresolved problems in the twenty-first century. Popes John Paul
II, Benedict XVI, and Francis have commented on the continued
urgency of these issues.

Urbanization. Industrial growth, population expansion, and
the attraction of big cities brings about great concentrations of
population—sometimes millions. Meanwhile, industrialization
allows certain businesses to develop while others die or move.
Thus, new social problems are created: professional or regional
unemployment, the movement of workers, the elimination
of some jobs and creation of others by changes in technology,
uneven conditions in various branches of industry. Unlimited
competition with modern advertising methods and e-commerce
via the Internet incessantly launches new products and tries to
attract new consumers while other industrial plants, still capable
of functioning, become useless. Large areas of the population
cannot satisfy their primary needs while superfluous needs are
cleverly created.

New working classes are born in the heart of the cities sometimes
abandoned by the rich. They form a belt of misery, a silent protest

against the luxury, consumption, and waste they see so near to them. The big city can foster discrimination and indifference. It lends itself to new forms of exploitation and domination. Misery spreads where human dignity flounders amid delinquency, violence, criminality, and abuse of drugs and sex.

There is an urgent need to reweave the social fabric so that humans can develop and improve themselves and their conditions, while still providing for their needs. Cultural centers must be created or developed at the community or parish levels. Christians must discover new modes of neighborliness, apply social justice in an original manner, and take responsibility for our common future.

The Role of Women. There is lively demand for an end to discrimination of women and for establishing equal rights. In pursuing these aims, we must take care to prevent a false equality that would deny women the opportunity to choose to fulfill their historical roles at the heart of the family and of society. Legislation and our Christian attitude should protect women, their independence as individuals, and their equal rights to participate in cultural, economic, political, and social life.

Workers. Every individual has a right to work, to develop qualities and personality in the exercise of a profession, and to receive a just wage which will enable families to lead a worthy life on the material, social, cultural, and spiritual level. Workers must have the right to provide for medical insurance and for assistance with needs arising from advancing years. The important role of union organizations must be recognized—the representation of workers who are working together for economic advancement of society and a responsibility for the common good. But the temptation arises to impose, especially by strikes, conditions which may be detrimental to the overall economy and society.

We must never forget that the purpose of work at our jobs is to use our God-given talents and to make a living, not to make a killing. With this in mind we will remember that just wages mean fair wages for workers at both ends of the salary scale, not colossal paychecks and tremendous perks at one end of the scale and meager, subsistence-level pay at the other end.

Franciscans affirm the position of Jesus and Francis that individuals have worth not because of what they can produce but because of who they are in the eyes of God.

Victims of Change. Discernment is needed to strike at the roots of new situations of injustice. In an industrial society with its constant and rapid change, more and more people are personally disadvantaged. The Church directs her attention to these new "poor"—the disabled and mentally challenged, older people, various minority groups, the working poor—in order to recognize them, help them, and defend their place and dignity in a society hardened by competition.

The rights of workers to maintain benefits of health care and retirement benefits must be protected, particularly when corporate downsizing and restructuring create job losses.

Discrimination. Among victims of injustice must be placed those who are discriminated against because of their race, ethnic origin, culture, sex, sexual orientation, or religion. Racial and ethnic discrimination is an injustice particularly important in our times, creating tension around the world. All members of the human race share the same basic rights and duties and the same eternal destiny. All should be equal before the law, find equal admittance to economic, cultural, civic, and social life and should benefit from a fair sharing of the nation's riches and opportunities.

Immigrant Workers. Many immigrant workers have difficulty in becoming socially established in their adopted country even though they provide it with essential labor. These workers should be integrated and provision made for their personal and professional advancement, and access to decent housing where their families can join them.

The Media. Those in the media have a serious moral responsibility to the truth, to the needs and reactions they generate and the values they put forward. We all have a serious moral responsibility to keep the media mindful of their role and to act to ensure that that responsibility is upheld.

The Environment. Our exploitation of nature carries grave risks to health and life for ourselves and our entire planet. We must be aware of how our everyday choices can contribute to the destruction of the environment. Do we waste the energy of which our society is a disproportionate consumer? Do we reduce our consumption, reuse what we can, and recycle as much as possible? Do we seek ways to simplify our lifestyles that will help produce a healthier environment?

QUESTIONS FOR REFLECTION

- What basic Christian principles are involved in the discussion of these problems?
- Does the Church—and do individual Christians—bear responsibility to help solve them?

CONNECTING WITH SCRIPTURE

The Passover of the Jews was near, and Jesus went up to Jerusalem. In the temple he found people selling cattle, sheep, and doves, and the money-changers seated at their tables. Making a whip of cords, he drove all of them out of the temple, both the sheep and the cattle. He also poured out the coins of the money-changers and overturned their tables. He told those who were selling the doves, "Take these things out of here! Stop making my Father's house a market-place!" His disciples remembered that it was written, "Zeal for your house will consume me." The Jews then said to him, "What sign can you show us for doing this?" Jesus answered them, "Destroy this temple, and in three days I will raise it up." The Jews then said, "This temple has been under construction for forty-six years, and will you raise it up in three days?" But he was speaking of the temple of his body. After he was raised from the dead, his disciples remembered that he had said this; and they believed the scripture and the word that Jesus had spoken.

—John 2:13–22

CONNECTING WITH FRANCISCAN WRITINGS

And then, if we can do that, love those people who are not really enemies, we can even be led to love those who really hate us, who persecute us, who blame us. In our world today, there are a lot of people like that; maybe some of them even hate us because they have good reason to. Many of us have a way of life that a lot of people can't—people who hardly have enough to eat, who don't have the material things that we do, who don't have the freedom we have in our lives. They have reason to hate us. Maybe instead of getting all upset when some people in those circumstances rebel and get mean, we might try to understand that they're simply rebelling from a situation that is oppressing and demeaning and dehumanizing them.

As we look at the world today, for example, we see people who own companies in other countries. The owners are wealthy, yet they give the workers less than a living wage, sometimes making their employees work in oppressive conditions, simply to be profitable at the expense of the workers. Here we can't only love the people being oppressed, but we must love even their oppressors. These are the people Jesus tells us to love. Can I love them into a new vision of the world in which they see the most important thing is not profit, but human beings?

—Hilarion Kistner, *The Gospels According to Saint Francis*

APPLICATION TO DAILY LIFE

- Name some concrete examples of injustice suffered by the poor. Choose one situation and decide on one simple thing you can do to bring justice.
- Decide on a practical way in which you can simplify your way of living and, in doing so, help the environment.

PRAYER

Creator God, you commanded your creation
to be fertile and multiply, and we did.
We are many, and so often we can't get along with one another.
Families split, citizens argue and fight, countries war.
In the midst of conflict, help us to live your solution to our social problems:
"Love one another as I have loved you."
Amen.

....

The Practice of Justice

"And every member is to give the treasurer one ordinary denar. The treasurer is to collect this money and distribute it on the advice of the ministers among the poor brothers and sisters, especially the sick and those who may have nothing for their funeral services; and thereupon among other poor; and they are to offer something of the money to the church."

—St. Francis, First Rule of the Third Order,

1221

One of the important documents in the Church's tradition on social justice is Justice in the World, issued by the Synod of Bishops called by Pope Paul in 1971. The third chapter of that document, entitled "The Practice of Justice," recognizes that those who venture to speak to people about justice must first be just themselves.

Rights must be preserved within the Church for those who serve her. Those who are associated with the Church should receive a sufficient livelihood via fair wages and a system for promotion to enjoy the social security that is customary in their region.

The Church recognizes everyone's right to suitable freedom of expression and thought. This includes the right of everyone to be heard in a spirit of dialogue that preserves legitimate diversity within the Church.

It must never happen that the Gospel witness of the Church be clouded by the material riches we possess no matter how we use them. The same must be said about the privileges the Church has. Our faith demands of us a certain sparingness in the use of things. We should live and administer our goods in such a way that the Good News is convincingly proclaimed to the poor. If the Church appears to be identified with the rich and powerful of the world, its credibility is diminished or lost.

Bishops, priests, religious, laity—all must examine their lifestyles. Does belonging to the Church put us on a rich island in the midst of poverty? In our affluent society, does our lifestyle give an example of that sparingness in consumption which we claim to be necessary in order to feed millions of hungry people in the world?

The basic principles whereby the Gospel life can make itself felt in contemporary social life are to be found in the body of teaching set forth in the documents of Vatican II and in the social encyclicals:

Gaudium et Spes: "Pastoral Constitution on the Church in the Modern World"

Apostolicam Actuositatem: "Decree on the Apostolate of the Laity"

Laborem Exercens: "On Human Work"

Christifidelis Laici: "The Vocation and Mission of the Lay Faithful in the Church and the World"

"The Condition of Labor," Pope Leo XIII

"Reconstructing the Social Order," Pope Pius XI

"Christianity and Social Progress and Peace on Earth," Pope John XXIII

"Development of Peoples and Call to Action," Pope Paul VI

"The Church in the Modern World," Vatican II

"Justice in the World," 1971 Synod document

Laudato Si: On Care for Our Common Home" Pope Francis

Welcome or unwelcome, the Word of God should be present in the center of human situations. Our statements should always be in harmony with the circumstances of place and time and be a true expression of the faith. Our mission also demands that we denounce injustice, with charity, prudence, and firmness and in sincere dialogue with all parties concerned.

Finally, the liturgy can greatly serve education for justice, helping us discover the teaching of the prophets and the Lord and the apostles on the subject of justice. Preparation for Baptism is the beginning of the formation of the Christian conscience. The practice of Reconciliation should emphasize the social dimension of sin and of the sacrament. The Eucharist forms the community and places it at the service of humankind.

The power of the Spirit is continuously at work in the world. The people of God are present among the poor and those who suffer persecution and oppression. The body of Christ, the Church, lives in its own flesh, the passion of Christ, and bears witness to all people of his Resurrection.

The radical transformation of the world in the paschal mystery gives full meaning to the efforts of people to lessen injustice, violence, and hatred and to advance together in justice, freedom, brotherhood, and love.

QUESTIONS FOR REFLECTION

• How can Franciscans cooperate with the stated aims of the Church's teaching on social justice?

• How can you work toward these aims?

CONNECTING WITH SCRIPTURE

"You are the salt of the earth; but if salt has lost its taste, how can its saltiness be restored? It is no longer good for anything, but is thrown out and trampled under foot.

"You are the light of the world. A city built on a hill cannot be hidden. No one after lighting a lamp puts it under the bushel basket, but on the lampstand, and it gives light to all in the house. In the same way, let your light shine before others, so that they may see your good works and give glory to your Father in heaven."

—Matthew 5:13–16

CONNECTING WITH FRANCISCAN WRITINGS

Francis of Assisi became a lover of the Word. Although he was especially attuned to hearing the Word of God through the reading of the Scriptures, Francis knew the Scriptures to be the living Word of God, and this Word pulled him into the current of created living beings. Francis found God in the cloister of creation. His love and understanding of the Incarnation, the Word made flesh, grew by touching, tasting and seeing the good things of Creation.

—Ilia Delio, *Care for Creation*

APPLICATION TO DAILY LIFE

- Choose one of the Church's social teaching documents to read this week.
- Learn about or cooperate in some project to promote justice and peace.

PRAYER

Lord, to truly practice justice in your world
I must see circumstances from not just my point of view
but from the perspective of others—
the poor, the uneducated, the imprisoned, the persecuted.
Please, Lord, give me a broader vision of your world
and the courage to become an instrument of change.
Amen.

REFLECTION (4 0)

Blessed Are the Peacemakers

"The Lord revealed to me a salutation, that we
should say: 'The Lord give you peace.'"
—St. Francis of Assisi, *The Testament*

F rancis was an extremely simple man who understood the very
heart of life. We know that the desire for peace is one of the
deepest desires of the heart of man—and of Christ. Wherever
Francis went, he would greet people with, "The Lord give you
peace!" And he meant it!

Francis lived the beatitudes of our Lord. "Blessed are the poor
in spirit" was the wellspring of his sanctity. "Blessed are the
peacemakers" was the light of his apostolate. Because these words
were in the Gospel, he wanted them to be a special rule of life for
all his brothers and sisters. Since the time of Francis, the greeting
of Franciscans has been "Peace and all good things to you!" The
memory of Francis can add a rich warmth to this greeting among
Franciscans and as Franciscans greet others.

Peace is not simply pleasantness or the absence of problems,
temptation, or suffering. Christ had peace on the cross, and Mary
had peace when she lost her son. The Church has peace even
though it must suffer. St. Augustine called peace the "tranquility
of order." He believed that real peace depended on everything
being in its proper order. If our lives are governed by the laws of
God's love, our relationship with God as well as with others is
peaceful. No matter what the disturbances on the surface of our
life, as Christians, we can be peaceful with an inner serenity that
nothing can take from us. Truly virtuous living is the key to peace.

The peacemaker must be humble. When people are at each other's throats, they are in no mood to be lectured, but they may be melted by the quiet presence of one from whom they have nothing to fear. Peacemakers are not trying to impose their will on anybody or gain the reputation of being clever arbiters. Rather, they are protecting truth and goodness, trying to create a little breathing space for God's love. The peacemaker must be prudent and patient. St. Paul says: "If it is possible, so far as it depends on you, live peaceably with all" (Romans 12:18). One must be ready to be silent when words are futile, forgiving when sarcasm would be the most satisfying, and patient when there is every reason to give up.

The kind of peace Christ gives may sometimes be bought only at the price of pain. The result of Christ's teaching will at times bring us face-to-face with malicious opposition. The peace of goodwill, which only God can give, will always be the mark of his children. Francis did not have peace with his own father, but he had the peace of Christ.

QUESTIONS FOR REFLECTION

- What is the secret of peacemaking?
- How are those who follow Francis called in a special way to make peace their mission?

CONNECTING WITH SCRIPTURE

You have heard that it was said, "An eye for an eye and a tooth for a tooth." But I say to you, Do not resist an evildoer. But if anyone strikes you on the right cheek, turn the other also; and if anyone wants to sue you and take your coat, give your cloak as well; and if anyone forces you to go one mile, go also the second mile. Give to everyone who begs from you, and do not refuse anyone who wants to borrow from you.

You have heard that it was said, "You shall love your neighbor and hate your enemy." But I say to you, Love your enemies and pray for those who persecute you, so that you may be children of your Father in heaven; for he makes his sun rise on the evil and on the good, and sends rain on the righteous and on the unrighteous. For if you love those who love you, what reward do you have? Do not even the tax collectors do the same? And if you greet only your brothers and sisters, what more are you doing than others? Do not even the Gentiles do the same? Be perfect, therefore, as your heavenly Father is perfect.

—Matthew 5:38–48

CONNECTING WITH FRANCISCAN WRITINGS

He was terrified when he had finally been ushered into the Sultan's presence, and he wondered about all that equanimity stuff the saints were supposed to have had whenever a crisis arose. But he marched steadily forward, never dropping his eyes and staring openly into the Sultan's iron eyes. Francis was shaken by the scowl on the Sultan's face. He reminded Francis a little of his own father, that fierce concentration in his eyes, the drooping jowls, and the long oval ears.

As Francis drew nearer, the Sultan's expression changed to one of mild amusement. Francis couldn't help returning the expression. This seemed to please the Sultan because when Francis stopped in front of him, the two were grinning at each other. The sycophants around the Sultan were also grinning broadly until the Sultan turned and frowned; then they frowned back like little mirrors.

"Well, little man, I see you have courage. I watched your nervous walk and steady eyes, and I said to myself, him I would like at my court. He would tell me the truth, and not what I usually hear."

He emphasized the last few words, his eyes roaming coldly over his own courtiers. Francis said nothing. "I see you also have manners. I like that."

There was a long pause, embarrassing only to the courtiers who shifted from foot to foot and coughed tensely.

"Well, holy man, what do you want of me?"

"Only to bring you peace, great one."

The Sultan smiled. "But I like war, little Italian. For Allah I am conquering the world. It is why I was born and why I am Allah's instrument."

"But, great Prince, I am not talking about peace as the opposite of war. I speak of peace in your heart, a deep satisfaction and joy that flows from within like a rich wine."

"And what, to a warrior, can bring more inner peace than victory on the battlefield?"

"Prayer, O child of Allah."

"Prayer? And do I not pray every day to Allah?"

"More, I am sure, great leader, than many Christians pray."

"But I want to share with you a prayer I learned by fighting the great battle with myself, by conquering one by one the demons in my own heart. Your prayer is good, I am sure, but I want to teach you a new prayer."

"Then pray it for me now, here in front of these dullards who infest my tent."

Francis knelt down and lifted up his eyes, beyond the dais to a small opening in the tent that let the light in.

"You are Good, all Good, supreme Good,

Lord God, living and true."

The Sultan said nothing. He seemed moved by what Francis had poured from his heart. Yes, it was like a good rich wine. It was reminiscent of the Ninety-Nine Names of Allah. In a soft voice, so that only Francis could hear, he said. "Oh, little beggar and man of dreams. I wish in my heart that there were more gentle men like you to balance the hatred in the world.

Unfortunately, the world understands only two things: power and violence. Some day, your prayer says to me, the world will be turned upside down by little folk who fast and pray and who die rather than take up the sword. Till then, God's will is performed through men like me."

"Will you, Lord Sultan, pray for that day?"

"I will do more, honest man, I will let you walk out of this camp alive, so that you can pray for that day. I pray that after I am gone from this earth (but not before) Allah will change his mind and use meek instruments like you and that this great army of peace-loving beggars will outnumber the forces of hatred and violence. Go to your dreams, brave little man, and pray for me."

Then aloud the Sultan said, "Take this fool from our camp and give him safe passage to his own kind. I will not lower myself by harming beggars and vermin and threadbare Christians. You can see from the man's appearance how badly we have beaten down the Christians. Go."

He winked at Francis, and Francis smiled back, and in the strictest adherence to chivalrous conduct, backed out of the room. Just then the little boat came about and broke the rhythm of Francis' thoughts. His eyes focused in on the horizon again, and he saw the blessed land of Italy rising up before him. He was indeed home again even if, as a pilgrim and a stranger, he was not supposed to be at home anywhere. How deep the feelings lie, and no amount of preaching can change what is real and good, he thought.

—Murray Bodo, *Francis: The Journey and the Dream*

APPLICATION TO DAILY LIFE

- What are your obligations to peacemaking?
- Can you have peace in temptation? In suffering? In dryness of spirit?

- Remember, peace depends on truth. Stick with the facts in keeping peace. Help make peace in the neighborhood by letting rumors and gossip die when they reach you. For your own peace, try to be always in union with God.

PRAYER

You are Good, all Good, supreme Good,
Lord God, living and true.
You are love,
You are wisdom.
You are humility.
You are endurance.
You are rest.
You are peace
You are joy and gladness.
You are justice and moderation.
You are all our riches,
And you suffice for us.
You are beauty.
You are gentleness.
You are our protector.
You are our guardian and defender.
You are courage.
You are our haven and our hope.
You are our faith.
Our great consolation.
You are our eternal life,
Great and wonderful Lord,
God almighty,
Merciful Savior.

—St. Francis, "Praises of God"

REFLECTION (4 1)

Caring for Creation

"God looked at everything he had made, and he found it very good."

—Genesis 1:31

Moreover they should respect all creatures, animate and inanimate, which "bear the imprint of the Most High," and they should strive to move from the temptation of exploiting creation to the Franciscan concept of universal kinship.

—Rule of the Secular Franciscan Order, 18

St. Francis of Assisi was named the patron saint of ecology in 1989 for good reason. We might say that Francis saw with the eyes of God. He saw that all of creation was good, very good. Francis treasured each part of the created world that he viewed—from lofty Mt. Subasio where Assisi nestles to the tiniest worm creeping along the dusty road near his hometown. Francis believed that all creation was God's gift and was, therefore, to be treated as a treasure. In "The Canticle of the Creatures" Francis praises God for all creation—the sun and moon, the stars and the heavens, the wind and air, water and fire, flowers and fruits and herbs. Francis's heart overflowed with gratitude for all God's gifts.

Francis was following Jesus who also treasured creation to such an extent that he used creation images as the basis for explaining spiritual truths to those who flocked to him. He spoke of seeds and sheep, figs and fields, pearls and plants, wheat and water. He spoke of these elements of creation to bring people closer to God.

Think for a moment of your most treasured possession. How do you care for it? Perhaps you look at it lovingly and handle it with care. You thank the one who gave it to you. You consider its meaning in your life. You use it with reverence. You choose not to use it in ways that might destroy it. Such is the way we are called to reverence all of creation that God has entrusted to us for our use.

The Irish poet Oscar Wilde wrote, "Where there is sorrow there is holy ground." When we experience sorrow over polluted waterways, forests devastated by acid rain or over-logging, abandoned junk piles, air thick with industrial and automotive wastes, that may be the beginning of recreating such areas as "holy ground." From our observation of the present condition of the earth comes the beginnings of change in how we choose to use God's precious gift of creation.

No matter how little or how much material wealth we have at our disposal, we are called to use God's wisdom in determining how we spend it. We are not to judge others' ways but to thoughtfully, prayerfully consider how our habits affect the health of the earth. Then we must act in accord with the direction God gives us.

The Rule of the Secular Franciscan Order calls Franciscans to "universal kinship" with creation. That says we are all related to the universe and to each other. What is inflicted on the earth also wounds me and my family in some way through the chain of life that links us all. What is healed anywhere on the earth also promotes healing close to home.

QUESTIONS FOR REFLECTION

- What have you done recently to improve the corner of the earth where you live?
- What is enough for you in terms of money? Possessions? Housing?
- How do you understand "universal kinship" as important to your life?

CONNECTING WITH SCRIPTURE

O Lord, our Sovereign,
  how majestic is your name in all the earth!

You have set your glory above the heavens.
  Out of the mouths of babes and infants
you have founded a bulwark because of your foes,
  to silence the enemy and the avenger.

When I look at your heavens, the work of your fingers,
  the moon and the stars that you have established;
what are human beings that you are mindful of them,
  mortals that you care for them?

Yet you have made them a little lower than God,
  and crowned them with glory and honor.
You have given them dominion over the works of your hands;
  you have put all things under their feet,
all sheep and oxen,
  and also the beasts of the field,
the birds of the air, and the fish of the sea,
  whatever passes along the paths of the seas.

O Lord, our Sovereign,
  how majestic is your name in all the earth!

—Psalm 8:1–9

CONNECTING WITH FRANCISCAN WRITINGS

Rather than viewing the world from the top rung of the ladder of creation, Francis saw himself as part of creation. Poverty enabled him to realize his solidarity with creation. Instead of using creatures to ascend to God, he found God in all creatures and identified with them as brother and sister because he saw that they had the same primordial goodness as himself. By the end of his life, Francis considered himself as a brother to all creation.

All creation was his family. This was not some type of romantic love but a real insight: He found himself truly related to the stars, moon, sun, wind and earth. Everything spoke to him of God and he found God in and through created things.

—Ilia Delio, *Clare of Assisi*

APPLICATION TO DAILY LIFE

- Find out where your community's trash and garbage are discarded and visit the site. How can you reduce how much you contribute to this accumulation by reducing what you purchase, by reusing when possible and by recycling whatever materials you can?
- Walk in a park or a peaceful, natural setting while reminding yourself, "This is holy ground." Share your thoughts about this walk with a friend.
- What one thing can you begin to do differently today to preserve or restore a bit of creation?

PRAYER

All praise be yours, my Lord,
through Sister Earth, our mother,
who feeds us in her sovereignty
and produces various fruits with colored flowers and herbs.
Amen.

—St. Francis, "The Canticle of the Creatures"

Work: A Joint Venture in Creation

"Let them esteem work both as a gift and as a sharing in the creation, redemption and service of the human community."
—Rule of the Secular Franciscan Order, 16

If we're exhausted from a long day's difficult labor, we may question the notion that work is a gift. It may not always seem like a gift. However, consider the alternatives when one does not have the opportunity to work: unemployment, hopelessness, homelessness, inability to care for self and family. Those who face such conditions know how frightening it is not to be able to work. One of the frustrations of illness or injury is the inability to work in our usual manner.

When we work, we use the gifts God has given us. Perhaps a strong body is the gift that enables you to do manual labor. An inquisitive mind may lead you to become a scientist, teacher, or writer. A great sensitivity to people's needs may place you in social work or enable you to parent more effectively. Whatever work we do, as long as it does not cause scandal and does not lead us from being faithful followers of Jesus, is God's gift to us.

Gifts are not given to us for ourselves alone. I don't work to have more and more for me! Work is a gift we receive. Work is a gift we give. We use our gifts to continue God's work of creation and in doing so, God continues to create us.

As we begin each day, we can express thanks to God for the work before us, for the gift of talent that enables us to perform our work, for the people we will work with, for the results of our labor which we cannot yet see. If our work is not gratifying to us, we might ask God for the ability to develop our gifts in new directions. We must then be willing to work toward our own development through training and education.

When Francis heard God's call, it was "to go and rebuild [the] Church." Because Francis was not afraid of physical work, he immediately began to restore small churches in the Umbrian plain. He gathered and hauled stones, begged for other materials and used the strength of his muscle and the sweat of his brow to patch crumbling walls and replace collapsing roofs. He worked.

Later in his life, one might think that Francis had an aversion to work because he insisted that his little brothers beg for food and seek shelter in abandoned places rather than building houses for themselves, rather than earning a wage with which to go to the market or rent a place to live. However, the friars were encouraged to continue at whatever vocation they had pursued before becoming followers of Francis. For wages they were permitted to accept anything essential for their daily needs, except money. As married couples and those with families chose to follow the way of Francis, the restriction on receiving wages in the form of money was altered.

For Francis, work was gift to those for whom the labor was done. Wages in the form of food or clothing were gifts from those who benefited from the labor of Francis's followers. The friars were cautioned not to allow their work to interfere with their spiritual lives. They "should work in a spirit of faith and devotion and avoid idleness, which is the enemy of the soul, without however extinguishing the spirit of prayer and devotion, to which every temporal consideration must be subordinate" (St. Francis).

The places where we work are the places we are called to live "Gospel to life, life to the Gospel." We live the Gospel where we work, and where we work challenges us to learn the Gospel way more fully. The wages received in return for work performed can be used in creative ways for the betterment of others who may be less fortunate than we are. Earning a living is an honorable way of life, a way of using one's God-given gifts. To work is to become cocreator with God.

Francis made his work his play. Walking along the roads of Umbria, Francis spread his charism of joy. He sang—often in French, the language of the troubadours he admired—as he went to tend the lepers in their isolated hideaways. He played his imaginary fiddle made of sticks as he went from town to town preaching the Gospel he so loved. He was doing God's work! Perhaps if we think of our work as our way of doing God's work, if we think of our work as our play, we will find more joy in serving as workers. We might sing songs of praise on our daily commute to work. We may pray silent prayers of joyful thanksgiving throughout the day. We might look for opportunities to smile at others and to laugh with coworkers or customers. We can become Francis in our own marketplaces.

QUESTIONS FOR REFLECTION

• How does your attitude at work reflect your Christian way of life?
• What excuses do you make for not living in a Christian way?
• How do joyful coworkers empower you to work in a more productive, joyful way?

CONNECTING WITH SCRIPTURE

Now we command you, beloved, in the name of our Lord Jesus Christ, to keep away from believers who are living in idleness and not according to the tradition that they received from us. For you yourselves know how you ought to imitate us; we were not idle when we were with you, and we did not eat anyone's bread without paying for it; but with toil and labor we worked night and day, so that we might not burden any of you. This was not because we do not have that right, but in order to give you an example to imitate. For even when we were with you, we gave you this command: Anyone unwilling to work should not eat. For we hear that some of you are living in idleness, mere busybodies, not doing any work. Now such persons we command and exhort in the Lord Jesus Christ to do their work quietly and to earn their own living. Brothers and sisters, do not be weary in doing what is right.

—2 Thessalonians 3:6–13

CONNECTING WITH FRANCISCAN WRITINGS

The touch of the grain of wood, the feel of the plants to the hand, the brush of wheat shocks against the leg. All these real and natural things Francis loved. Toward the end of his life he dictated his last will, his Testament, to Brother Leo and he wanted to put everything he had learned into those last encouraging words to his brothers.

"This line, Brother Leo, is most important to me. So write it tenderly, write it well: 'I worked with my hands and I want all my brothers to work with their hands.'"

Francis remembered the melancholy times when depression had settled down and moved in like an unwanted guest that you don't know how to get rid of. He would then roll up his sleeves and plunge himself into exhausting physical work. He saw himself carrying, one by one, the large stones that were to hold up the crumbling St. Mary of the Angels, the little church that he loved so much. As he placed one stone upon another, the order of stone on stone seemed to order the chaos within. And when the last rock was mortared into place, Francis felt secure. He had accomplished something; he had built order, he had won the battle against confusion and despair.

...

The anxiety of wanting work, but finding none, always left him empty and feeling useless. And he would have to slow down and remind himself of Jesus' promise to provide for him even more than he had for the lilies of the field. Sometimes he would see lilies shriveled up or birds dead by the side of the road, and he would be afraid. His only comfort then was that the birds and lilies had not worried about their deaths beforehand. He should not either if he wanted to be free. Death would come when it would come, and he would cease upon some moment of ecstasy like a high-flying lark, shot in midair and crashing to the ground. His spirit would then leave the feathers behind and soar back in the blue cloudless skies of freedom, knowing he was now eternally immune to the arrows of any suffering or pain or death.

Francis had hoped that his moment of ecstasy would be while he was working in a field. But Brother Ass, as he always called his body, gave out too soon, and he had been unable to work for some time now. Ironically, this nonactivity was the hardest work he had ever done. For now nothing remained but love, kept alive by his faith and his hope. He had never been so utterly dependent on others. This was Lady Poverty's last courtship of him, and he realized for the first time that honeymoons do recur to those who persevere in love to the end. He now submitted finally and totally to his Lady, giving up for her even the pride of honest labor. And he was at peace in her arms.

—Murray Bodo, *Francis: The Journey and the Dream*

APPLICATION TO DAILY LIFE

- For a week, keep a record of what brings you joy in your work and what robs you of joy. Give thanks for the former; ask God's help with the latter. Each day, ask yourself how your work has contributed to God's ongoing creation of the world.

• Reflect on how work is used to set people free or to imprison them. What can you do to make a difference where individuals are prisoners to their work?

PRAYER

Dear God, when I'm tired from a day's work,
help me to remember that work is your gift.
I am graced with the privilege of toil
which continues your work of creation.
Thank you for the skills and talents
you have given me for my work.
Amen.

Charity for the Sick

"The 'Canticle of [the Creatures],' for all the depth it displays towards creatures, is nonetheless an earnest prayer. What makes it all the more remarkable is the fact that, written though it was during his last illness and amid intense suffering, it displays a heart filled with joy and happiness and a heart filled with the deepest gratitude toward almighty God, even for suffering and for Sister Death."

—Marion A. Habig, *St. Francis of Assisi: Omnibus of Sources*

In themselves, sickness and suffering are tragic and senseless. But Christ has sanctified even the wounds of human nature. This terrible scourge can be changed into a blessing by being united to the sufferings of Christ. Many people feel that this sublime privilege does not count for them. They are not good enough. Their sickness is not that important. They believe it is a punishment. But Christ wants to take your individual suffering and unite it to his. Of all the statements about our continuing Christ's life, none is more astounding that this: "I am now rejoicing in my sufferings for your sake, and in my flesh I am completing what is lacking in Christ's afflictions for the sake of his body, that is, the church" (Colossians 1:24). Francis received the highest proof of Christ's love and need of him when his body was literally put on a cross with Christ by the reality of the five wounds of the stigmata.

The Son of God entered into the human misery that had resulted from sin. He let evil seem to overcome him, going down even into death like anyone else. But the human Christ who did this was totally possessed by the love of his Father and this love was infinitely more powerful than all the forces of evil. Christ maintained his perfect trust no matter what happened to him. He was totally in the hands of his Father.

All the suffering brothers and sisters of Christ are asked to become part of Christ's great act of love on the cross by continuing it and offering it as a substitute for all the sins ever committed. "Beloved, do not be surprised at the fiery ordeal that is taking place among you to test you, as though something strange were happening to you. But rejoice insofar as you are sharing Christ's sufferings, so that you may also be glad and shout for joy when his glory is revealed" (1 Peter 4:12–13).

Franciscan tradition calls us to maintain the spirit of Francis especially in suffering. Those who are sick, disabled or afflicted with any infirmity are not to see these afflictions as punishments of God but as results of living in physical human bodies. We are to seek healing offered through the skills of the medical profession, which are also God's gifts. We are to call on the prayers of the community for healing. We can request the Anointing of the Sick. And in the manner of Francis, we will remember these words in order to maintain our sense of joy even in suffering: "I beg the sick brother to thank God for everything and to desire to be whatever the Lord wills, whether sick or well" (the Rule of 1221).

St. Francis showed his tender regard for the sick by making an exception in one of his strictest rules:

> Let none of the brothers, therefore, wherever he may be or go, carry, receive, or have received in any way coin or money, whether for clothing, books, or payment for some work—indeed, not for any reason, unless for an evident need of the sick brothers.... They must rejoice when they

live among people considered of little value and looked down upon, among the poor and the powerless, the sick and the lepers....

If any of the brothers falls sick, wherever he may be, let the other brothers not leave him behind unless one of the brothers, or even several of them, if necessary, is designated to serve him as "they would want to be served themselves." ... I beg the sick brother to thank God for everything (the Rule of 1221).

Francis saw Jesus in the Gospels not only preaching the kingdom to people's minds and hearts but also going out of his way to relieve the pain and sickness of their bodies. And Francis could do no less! Nothing could be closer to the mind of Francis than to see Christ in the sick and to relieve his pain.

QUESTIONS FOR REFLECTION
• What can Christians do for those who are sick?
• What is offered to God in times of suffering?

CONNECTING WITH SCRIPTURE
Are any among you suffering? They should pray. Are any cheerful? They should sing songs of praise. Are any among you sick? They should call for the elders of the church and have them pray over them, anointing them with oil in the name of the Lord. The prayer of faith will save the sick, and the Lord will raise them up; and anyone who has committed sins will be forgiven.

—James 5:13–15

CONNECTING WITH FRANCISCAN WRITINGS
Compassion requires a depth of soul, a connectedness of soul to earth, an earthiness of person to person, and a flow of love from heart to heart. To evolve toward the fullness of Christ we must be

able to love the weak, the unlovable, the fragile, and lame. The Body of Christ becomes one when we ourselves create bridges of love. The compassionate person walks across the bridge into the life of another saying along the way, "you are not alone, I am with you."

—Ilia Delio, *Compassion*

APPLICATION TO DAILY LIFE

- Whether healthy or sick, try to see suffering and sickness in its union with the suffering and victorious Christ. Try to visit at least one sick or homebound person this week. Bring a small gift. Offer your services for a task the individual may need done.

PRAYER

Lord, your life on earth was filled with concern for the sick.
Have compassion now on all who share your pain.
Give them healing of mind and body;
restore their strength and spirit.
May they be comforted by the knowledge
that we are praying for them
and find peace in a sense of your presence.
May they know that, in a special way, they are united with your suffering.
May they contribute to the welfare of the whole people of God
by associating themselves freely with your passion and death
for the salvation of the world.
Bless those who take care of the sick.
In their own time of need, may they receive a hundredfold
the blessings they have given.
Amen.

—Leonard Foley, *Prayers for Caregivers*

"Repair My Church"

"When he heard that Christ's disciples should not possess gold or silver or money, or carry on their journey a wallet or a sack, nor bread...but that they should preach the kingdom of God and penance, the holy man, Francis, immediately exulted in the spirit of God. 'This is what I want,' he said, 'this is what I seek, this is what I desire with all my heart.'"

— Thomas of Celano, *The Life of St. Francis*

One of the great turning points of Francis's life was the occasion when Christ spoke to him from the crucifix. He had been walking near the little church of San Damiano. He was sad at its crumbling, unkempt condition and went in to pray before the altar. As he prayed, he heard a voice speaking to him from the crucifix: "Francis, go and repair my Church which as you see is wholly in ruin."

He was startled. His Master had spoken to him! He took the words to mean the poor little church on that spot, and in his humility he quickly replied, "Gladly, Lord, will I repair it." If the rest of his life had been spent doing nothing but repairing the stones of that or any dilapidated church, he would have been supremely happy. It was nothing, but it was for the Lord. It was only later that it became evident that it was the Church of Christ that Francis was to repair, not physical structures but the spiritual foundation.

Great benefits to the Church would come from this ragged band of Gospel minstrels who gathered around Francis. But the Holy

Father was at first repulsed when Francis came to him. It was almost against his will that he finally was attracted to the poor little man from Assisi. He remembered a dream which he had. The Mother Church of Christendom, Saint John Lateran, was tottering on its foundations. A religious person, small of stature and unimpressive in appearance, came and held it up by setting his back against it. The pope realized that Francis was this man and gave the first approval to the new Order.

The Church is ourselves, Christ united with his members. We are the glory and the shame of the Church. The constant purification of the Church, therefore, must be done by those who make up the Church and who need purification, that is, by you and me. We spoil what God has made. Therefore, the purifying, too, must begin in ourselves. Even our penance is not a private affair. We are all in this together, allowing God to purify and reform us and others and the Church.

Perhaps the greatest reform needed in the Church today is the acceptance of the idea of reform. Vatican II began in a blaze of glory, but its promise and ideals have not substantially changed the attitude of many Catholics. Decades later, polarization between liberals and conservatives, new and old emphases in theology, and similar issues continue to be scandals in the Church. If there was ever a peacemaking task, it is in building up harmony where differences threaten to divide the Church.

"We are sent," says St. Francis, "to heal the wounds, to tend the maimed, and to bring back those who have lost their way." As long as there is one sinner on earth, Francis would be restless.

We should show a special kindness to those who have strayed from the Church—whether because of misunderstanding, anger, marriage issues, or any other reason. The farther they are from the Church, the more they need the kindness of Christ. The friendly greeting of one Catholic may be the only link with the faith of their childhood. God can use this as a grace to bring them back. It may take many years, but charity never fails.

On one occasion when Francis became discouraged, Christ said to him, "Tell me, you simple and ignorant little man, why do you grieve so when a brother leaves the Order and the brothers do not follow the way I showed you? Tell me, then, who has founded this community? Who converts them to penitence?" It is Christ alone who is the missionary. He works through us, and he succeeds only to the degree that he can create his life in us first.

QUESTIONS FOR REFLECTION

• What actually is the Good News? How is it proclaimed within the Church?

CONNECTING WITH SCRIPTURE

Now all the tax collectors and sinners were coming near to listen to him. And the Pharisees and the scribes were grumbling and saying, "This fellow welcomes sinners and eats with them."

So he told them this parable: "Which one of you, having a hundred sheep and losing one of them, does not leave the ninety-nine in the wilderness and go after the one that is lost until he finds it? When he has found it, he lays it on his shoulders and rejoices. And when he comes home, he calls together his friends and neighbors, saying to them, 'Rejoice with me, for I have found my sheep that was lost.' Just so, I tell you, there will be more joy in heaven over one sinner who repents than over ninety-nine righteous persons who need no repentance.

"Or what woman having ten silver coins, if she loses one of them, does not light a lamp, sweep the house, and search carefully until she finds it? When she has found it, she calls together her friends and neighbors, saying, 'Rejoice with me, for I have found the coin that I had lost.' Just so, I tell you, there is joy in the presence of the angels of God over one sinner who repents."

—Luke 15:1–10

CONNECTING WITH FRANCISCAN WRITINGS

I see clearly...that the thing the church needs most today is the ability to heal wounds and to warm the hearts of the faithful; it needs nearness, proximity. I see the church as a field hospital after battle. It is useless to ask a seriously injured person if he has high cholesterol and about the level of his blood sugars! You have to heal his wounds. Then we can talk about everything else. Heal the wounds, heal the wounds.... And you have to start from the ground up.

...

How are we treating the people of God? I dream of a church that is a mother and shepherdess. The church's ministers must be merciful, take responsibility for the people and accompany them like the good Samaritan, who washes, cleans and raises up his neighbor. This is pure Gospel. God is greater than sin. The structural and organizational reforms are secondary—that is, they come afterward. The first reform must be the attitude. The ministers of the Gospel must be people who can warm the hearts of the people, who walk through the dark night with them, who know how to dialogue and to descend themselves into their people's night, into the darkness, but without getting lost.

—Pope Francis, "A Big Heart Open to God," *America*

APPLICATION TO DAILY LIFE

- Are you "old Church" or "new Church?" Are you willing to listen to others' views of the Church?
- Read your parish bulletin and seriously consider offering your services in an area where you can help strengthen your community of the faithful.

PRAYER

I'm listening, Lord Jesus.
What part of your Church
would you have me rebuild?
Show me the way.
Amen.

That All May Be One

> "I beseech all my brothers whether clergy or lay, whether engaged in preaching or in prayer or in labor, to aim at keeping humble in everything; not to boast, nor be pleased with themselves nor interiorly elated, at the good words or deeds, or anything good which God says or does or accomplishes in them or through them."
>
> —St. Francis of Assisi

Most Catholics recognize those things that unite all Christians rather than the things that divide them. While it does not reflect perfect unity, it is to be treasured and reinforced. This is a much better focus than emphasizing our differences.

Many Catholics feel that they do not know enough to talk about religion. Others may think they know a great deal about their Church when, in fact, they have not learned about the faith since their school days. In either case, those who appreciate their faith will want to share it with others. People never tire of enthusiastically inviting others to a cause they deeply believe in.

Furthermore, we should be as much up-to-date as possible on the modern needs that call for principles for their solution. We should be aware of discussions and movements within the Church, the statements of the pope and the bishops. We should be conscious of the problems of the society in which we live. Principles do not change, but there are shifting sets of circumstances to which principles are to be applied.

Christianity is spread by the Holy Spirit. St. Paul said, "My speech and my proclamation were not with plausible words of wisdom, but with a demonstration of the Spirit and of power" (1 Corinthians 2:4). We do the faith more harm than good if we seem intent only on crushing opponents in arguments. Besides, arguments are useless when emotion is aroused.

We can do many things to spread the faith. Listen respectfully to others who ask about our faith. Explain beliefs and practices of the faith to those who ask. If you are full of the faith, you will unconsciously and automatically apply it lovingly to all situations. You will thus be preaching the Gospel without being preachy.

QUESTIONS FOR REFLECTION

• How can you spread the faith in ordinary conversation?
• Would an evangelical Christian be envious of your zeal?

CONNECTING WITH SCRIPTURE

I am the good shepherd. The good shepherd lays down his life for the sheep. The hired hand, who is not the shepherd and does not own the sheep, sees the wolf coming and leaves the sheep and runs away—and the wolf snatches them and scatters them. The hired hand runs away because a hired hand does not care for the sheep. I am the good shepherd. I know my own and my own know me, just as the Father knows me and I know the Father. And I lay down my life for the sheep. I have other sheep that do not belong to this fold. I must bring them also, and they will listen to my voice. So there will be one flock, one shepherd. For this reason the Father loves me, because I lay down my life in order to take it up again. No one takes it from me, but I lay it down of my own accord. I have power to lay it down, and I have power to take it up again. I have received this command from my Father.

—John 10:11–18

CONNECTING WITH FRANCISCAN WRITINGS

At the heart of it all, Franciscan prayer is about Gospel living. It is not really concerned with knowledge or intellectual contemplation. It is concerned with the human person and the transformation of the human person in god. It is about living Christ and making the Good News of the Incarnation alive. How desperately this path of prayer is needed in our world today! We seek healing of division, hate and violence. We desire wholeness, unity and peace. Haw shall these things come about? Are they merely ideas of values that must be given flesh and blood? To live the gospel is to put flesh and blood on God and proclaim throughout the universe, the glory of God is full alive! Without flesh and blood, the Good News that God has become human and healed the divisions of humankind and all creation is not news at all. Christian life demands human participation or it simply does not exist. It is an empty title in a broken world. If we desire justice, peace and love among humankind and throughout creation, then we human must become justice, peace and love.... We must descend with Christ into the darkness of our humanity so that we may rise with Christ in the unity of love. In a world marked by violence and death, suffering does not have the last word. The last word is love and that love is the fullness of Christ, the Word of God.

—Ilia Delio, *Franciscan Prayer*

APPLICATION TO DAILY LIFE

- Search for the proof that your belief in Christianity shows in your daily life. Can people where you work depend on you for straight information about the faith?

- Are you as well informed about your faith as about your job, fashions, cars, sports, entertainers, or the stock market? Do one thing this week to increase your awareness and knowledge of matters of faith and religion.

PRAYER

Someone I know needs you in their life, Lord.
Give me the faith and courage to speak up for you
and invite them into your love.
Amen.

Witness to the Gospel

"All Brothers ought to preach by their actions."
—St. Francis of Assisi, Rule of 1221

Living the Gospel can be described in many ways. Whether we are speaking of virtue or sin, it is true that attitude is all-important. We are what we decide to be, by an ongoing and basic decision. But it is also true that our deepest attitudes must express themselves, and they do. One does not keep up a good example long unless it is the fruit of a genuine inner commitment.

We sometimes think that we have little influence on others. They seem to pay little or no attention to us. Yet, let us look at our own lives. After the grace of God, all the goodness we have is the result of good example. We have been powerfully influenced by our mothers and fathers, teachers and friends, and the ever-widening circle of good people whom we meet in life. We are influenced by the example of those who have gone before us. We remember particular instances: being encouraged to pray by seeing a friend making the Way of the Cross, marveling at the silent endurance of injury by a friend, seeing silent and Christlike suffering, seeing a courageous defense of someone being persecuted.

We may be moved for the moment by some unusual and spectacular action of another. But the influences that affect us most deeply are those which continue day after day, year after year. Constant good example formed our characters. The sight of Dad going to Communion every Sunday is a picture that will never be forgotten and will never cease to encourage us to do the same. The memory of Mom taking dinner to a sick neighbor will inspire us to do the same.

Someone once said: "What you are thunders so loud, I can't hear what you say!" We can only influence others by what we are. We may playact for a while, but sooner or later everyone knows exactly what and who we are. We must examine our external conduct, but this will bring us face-to-face with our interior spirit. If we take care of the inner peace that comes from living close to Christ, we will have no trouble giving good example. When others see us, they will see Christ.

A story in one of the earliest biographies of Francis describes the power of his example and the great spirit that attracted everyone to him. At one of the meetings of the friars, it was said that "if one of the brothers was undergoing an inner struggle or fighting against a temptation, it sufficed for him to see St. Francis, to hear him speak with loving zeal, to witness the sacrifices he made— and all temptations and all sadness miraculously vanished, for he spoke to them with great compassion, not as a judge, but as a loving father to his sons, or a good physician to his patients" (*Legend of the Three Companions*).

We must fight the sinfulness of the world, but not by withdrawing from the conflict. We join, we become involved in, the activities of the world that we may put the spirit of Christ into them. In theaters and newspaper offices, in washrooms and supermarkets, in colleges and hospitals and restaurants, we must be Christ to everyone. We must be, in these circumstances, what Christ would be in them. We must do what he would do.

QUESTIONS FOR REFLECTION

- Who has influenced you the most in the way you live your life?
- What is it in others that encourages you to live your Christian life more faithfully?
- Whom are you influencing? How?

CONNECTING WITH SCRIPTURE

Beware of false prophets, who come to you in sheep's clothing but inwardly are ravenous wolves. You will know them by their fruits. Are grapes gathered from thorns, or figs from thistles? In the same way, every good tree bears good fruit, but the bad tree bears bad fruit. A good tree cannot bear bad fruit, nor can a bad tree bear good fruit. Every tree that does not bear good fruit is cut down and thrown into the fire. Thus you will know them by their fruits.

—Matthew 7:15–20

CONNECTING WITH FRANCISCAN WRITINGS

Toward the end of his life, Francis began to have great misgivings about the Order and the materialism and selfishness that he saw creeping into the brotherhood. One day he was so depressed about this state of affairs that he began to feel sorry for himself.

Always up, up, up. Never a hill down from somewhere. Francis wondered when that downhill moment would come, if ever. Christ had struggled so long and hard to be born in him and this concern over the brothers had lasted so many years that he even despaired at times of seeing the day of the Lord in his old age. That thought bothered him, too. Why did he consider himself old? Where had the joy gone that had made him young?

Francis knew, but hated to admit it, that he had succumbed to the greatest temptation of all: that of thinking that the Order was his. That he was in charge, instead of Christ. He had seen so many of his brothers grow bitter that way. And now he was in the same morass as they. He was beginning to feel possessive about his dreams again. Christ had given him everything, and now he was acting as though the Dream, the inspiration, was all his, and nobody had better dare tarnish his ideal, his original inspiration.

Francis broke out laughing at the irony of it all. That he could have come so far with Jesus and now revert to what he was when he was a cloth salesman in his father's shop. He wished Brother Leo were at his side now. Leo would tell him what a sinner he really was and how selfish this whole mess was. If only he had remembered that Jesus was almost as concerned about the brotherhood as he was! He remembered his pious words to the brothers that sadness and melancholy were the devil's work; and if any brother were dejected, he should go to confession. What a laugh! How different things look when you're the one who's depressed. The whole affair was becoming so funny that he thought he'd run outdoors and do something dumb like the old sillies he used to pull to keep the brothers guessing and to distract them from taking themselves too seriously.

So Francis left the hermitage and ran down the hillside. When he reached the bottom, he picked up two sticks and began playing little violin pieces for all the chipmunks in the whole wood.

—Murray Bodo, *Francis: The Journey and the Dream*

APPLICATION TO DAILY LIFE

- Perhaps our influence on others—children, friends, fellow workers, neighbors—is greater than we realize. Think of some action you have performed recently and consider how your act influenced others positively or negatively.
- Remember that if you allow God to possess your mind and heart, good example will take care of itself. Act on the knowledge that you influence people most by unfailing faithfulness to daily duties in the spirit of Christ.

PRAYER

Please, Lord, keep me from being a hypocrite.
I want to live my belief in you with honesty.
Show me the secret corners of my life
that I try to hide from others and from you.
Amen.

....

Perfect Joy

"May I never boast of anything except the cross
of Our Lord Jesus Christ."

—Galatians 6:14

A classic story comes from that delightful book of Franciscan tradition called the *Fioretti*—"The Little Flowers"—of St. Francis. It summarizes the spirit of Francis.

One winter day, St. Francis was returning to Saint Mary of the Angels from Perugia with Brother Leo. The bitter cold made them suffer keenly. St. Francis called to Brother Leo, who was walking a bit ahead of him and said: "Brother Leo, even if the Friars Minor in every country give a great example of holiness and integrity and good edification, nevertheless write down and note carefully that perfect joy is not in that."

And when he had walked on a bit, St. Francis called again saying: "Brother Leo, even if a Friar Minor gives sight to the blind, heals the paralyzed, drives out devils, gives hearing back to the deaf, makes the lame walk, and restores speech to the dumb, and what is still more, brings back to life a man who has been dead four days, write that perfect joy is not in that."

And going on a bit, Francis cried out again in a strong voice: "Brother Leo, if a Friar Minor knows all languages and all sciences and Scripture, if he also knows how to prophesy and to reveal not only the future but also the secrets of the consciences and minds of others, write down and note carefully that perfect joy is not in that."

And as they walked on, after a while Francis called again forcefully: "Brother Leo, Little Lamb of God, even if a Friar

Minor could speak with the voice of an angel and knew the courses of the stars and the powers of herbs and knew all about the treasures in the earth, and if he knew the qualities of birds and fishes, animals, humans, roots, trees, rocks and waters, write down and note carefully that true joy is not in that."

And going on a bit farther, St. Francis called again strongly: "Brother Leo, even if a Friar Minor could preach so well that he should convert all infidels to the faith of Christ, write that perfect joy is not there."

Now when he had been talking this way for a distance of two miles, Brother Leo in great amazement asked him: "Father, I beg you in God's name to tell me where perfect joy is."

And St. Francis replied: "When we come to Saint Mary of the Angels, soaked by the rain and frozen by the cold, all soiled with mud and suffering from hunger, and we ring at the gate of the place and the brother porter comes and says angrily: 'Who are you?' And we say: 'We are two of your brothers.' And he contradicts us, saying: 'You are not telling the truth. Rather you are two rascals who go around deceiving people and stealing what they give to the poor. Go away!' And he does not open for us, but makes us stand outside in the snow and rain, cold and hungry, until night falls—then if we endure all those insults and cruel rebuffs patiently, without being troubled and without complaining, and if we reflect humbly and charitably that the porter really knows us and that God makes him speak against us, oh, Brother Leo, write that perfect joy is there!

"And if we continue to knock, and the porter comes out in anger and drives us away with curses and hard blows like bothersome scoundrels, saying: 'Get away from here, you dirty thieves—go to the hospital! Who do you think you are? You certainly won't eat or sleep here!' and if we bear it patiently and take the insults with joy and love in our heart, Brother Leo, write that perfect joy is there!

"And if later, suffering intensely from hunger and painful cold, with night falling, we still knock and call, and crying loudly beg them to open for us and let us come in for the love of God, and he grows still more angry and says: 'Those fellows are bold and shameless ruffians. I'll give them what they deserve!'

"And he comes out with a knotty club, and grasping us by the cowl throws us onto the ground, rolling us in the mud and snow and beats us with the club so much that he covers our bodies with wounds—if we endure all those evils and insults and blows with joy and patience, reflecting that we must accept and bear the sufferings of the Blessed Christ patiently for love of him, oh, Brother Leo, write: that is perfect joy!

"And now hear the conclusion, Brother Leo. Above all the graces and gifts of the Holy Spirit which Christ gives to his friends is that of conquering oneself and willingly enduring sufferings, insults, humiliations, and hardships for the love of Christ. For we cannot glory in all those other marvelous gifts of God, as they are not ours but God's as the Apostle says: 'What have you that you have not received?'

"But we can glory in the cross of tribulations and afflictions, because that is ours, and so the Apostle says: 'I will not glory save in the Cross of Our Lord Jesus Christ!'"

QUESTIONS FOR REFLECTION
- What phrase sums up St. Francis's description of perfect joy?
- What is the motive to seeing perfect joy as Francis saw it?

CONNECTING WITH SCRIPTURE
Blessed are those who are persecuted for righteousness' sake, for theirs is the kingdom of heaven.

Blessed are you when people revile you and persecute you and utter all kinds of evil against you falsely on my account. Rejoice and be glad, for your reward is great in heaven, for in the same way they persecuted the prophets who were before you.

—Matthew 5:10–12

CONNECTING WITH FRANCISCAN WRITINGS

Prayer is the path to peace because it is the path to love, not to a "feel good" love but to compassionate love, the type of love that can reach out and feel for another and give itself to the other without asking for anything in return. It is in prayer that we encounter Jesus who is our peace and learn from him the way to peace. One of the most noted peacemakers of our time, Daniel Berrigan, wrote that "the soul of peacemaking is the will to give one's life." Bonaventure, too, saw that there is no other way to peace than through the burning love of the Crucified. Union with God is a union in love whereby one is inflamed with the desire of crucified love. In this union of love, a person is willing to suffer or die out of love for another, following the example of Christ.

—Ilia Delio, *Franciscan Prayer*

APPLICATION TO DAILY LIFE

- What is the greatest suffering you must endure today?
- What is your greatest personal cross?
- When a painful situation arises, try to remember the story of perfect joy and apply it as Christ inspires you to do.

PRAYER

True joy guides my life toward you, dear God.
Joy can come even in times of sadness
because you are with me in the pain and suffering.
You are my joy!
Amen.

....

PART FIVE

The Franciscan Family

The Franciscan family, as one among many spiritual families raised up by the Holy Spirit in the Church, unites all members of the People of God—laity, religious, and priests—who recognize that they are called to follow Christ in the footsteps of St. Francis of Assisi.

In various ways and forms but in life-giving union with each other, they intend to make present the charism of their common seraphic Father in the life and mission of the Church.

REFLECTION (48)

··

Community Life

"After the Lord gave me some brothers, no one showed me what I had to do, but the Most High Himself revealed to me that I should live according to the pattern of the Holy Gospel."

—St. Francis, "The Testament"

Francis as a young man treasured his relationships with his friends. They reveled together, partied together, even went to war together. When Francis discovered Lady Poverty and first heard the Lord's call to "go and rebuild [his] Church," he entered a period of aloneness. He left friends and family behind because he knew they could not understand his call. Indeed, at this time he did not understand it himself. Those who did not understand his need to search for meaning might hold him back, deter him from what was most important to him. During this period of his life, he meandered through the Umbrian countryside as a solitary wanderer, searching for understanding of his call from Jesus and seeking to know himself. Alone, he entered the caves of Mount Subasio to pray, perhaps to call out to God where no one else could hear his shouts of pain and confusion when the dream seemed unclear.

But Francis could not remain alone for two reasons. He enjoyed being with people. And he knew that Jesus in the Gospels also frequently spent time with others, whether his chosen disciples or the crows who gathered around him. Francis became a kind of human magnet as others observed his way of life and experienced his spiritual growth. He could not have remained alone if he had wanted to. The life he had chosen was simply too attractive to others who loved the Lord.

Bernard of Quintavalle was Francis's first follower. Bernard had what many people think of as essentials for happiness—wealth and a respected social position in the town of Assisi. But Bernard lacked the joy in life that he witnessed in the new Francis.

So, Bernard invited Francis to his home for supper and a night's rest, since Francis now had no home to call his own. As evening came, Francis feigned sleep, then spent the night in prayer. Witnessing, without Francis's knowing, the intensity and humility of his prayer, "My God and my all!" repeated through the night and dawn hours, Bernard knew Francis to be a genuine and faithful follower of the Lord. And with daybreak, Francis had his first follower.

Neither man knew that a religious movement across centuries and around the world would result from their friendship with each other and with Jesus. They were now simply two rather than one in love with Lady Poverty and setting out to rebuild the Church of Jesus Christ. Others clamored to be around them because they were good, they were joyful, they were men of God. The two became thousands. The unmarried men were joined by women, married men, families. If this had not happened, the Franciscan charism might have lingered a few years after Francis's death in 1226. It might have been captured in history books. It might have become a blessed memory in Church history. Instead the Franciscan way exists today, not in books and memories but in the lives of men, women, and children around the globe.

Those who are called to follow Francis are called to be brothers and sisters to Jesus with Francis and his other followers. This Franciscan community keeps us from becoming self-centered. It creates the place where apostolic work in the world is fostered. It gives us strength where we are weak. Gathering as a community gives us opportunities to love others with all their goodness as well as their flaws and irritating ways. And they can do the same for us. We have an intimate spiritual family within the larger spiritual family of Church where we can grow in holiness according to God's command, "You shall be holy, for I am holy" (1 Peter 1:16).

We travel the Franciscan way together, not as individuals on private journeys. Laughter and humor lighten life's burdens. We learn to resolve disagreements peaceably. We learn to forgive ourselves and others as we begin again and again to follow Francis and Jesus.

QUESTIONS FOR REFLECTION

- Why is community necessary to live the authentic Franciscan way of life?
- What aspects of Franciscan community life might be helpful to your faith journey?

CONNECTING WITH SCRIPTURE

Awe came upon everyone, because many wonders and signs were being done by the apostles. All who believed were together and had all things in common; they would sell their possessions and goods and distribute the proceeds to all, as any had need. Day by day, as they spent much time together in the temple, they broke bread at home and ate their food with glad and generous hearts, praising God and having the goodwill of all the people. And day by day the Lord added to their number those who were being saved.

—Acts 2:46–47

CONNECTING WITH FRANCISCAN WRITINGS

Compassion is realized when we know ourselves related to one another, a deep relatedness of our humanity despite our limitations. It goes beyond the differences that separate us and enters the shared space of created being. To enter this space is to have space within ourselves, to welcome into our lives the stranger, the outcast, and the poor. Love is stronger than death and the heart that no longer fears death is truly free. Compassion flourishes when we have nothing to protect and everything to share. It is the gravity of all living beings that binds together all that is weak and limited into a single ocean of love.

We have the capacity to heal this earth of its divisions, its wars, its violence, and its hatreds. This capacity is the love within us to suffer with one another and to love the other without reward. Love that transcends the ego is love that heals. When we lose ourselves for the sake of love, we shall find ourselves capable of real love. Compassion flows best from a heart open, free, and deeply in love with life. It rises above the individual and yearns for oneness of heart.

—Ilia Delio, *Compassion: Living in the Spirit of St. Francis*

APPLICATION TO DAILY LIFE

- If you are searching for a Franciscan community, ask Franciscans in your area for more information. You might want to visit a nearby Franciscan parish or find a Secular Franciscan group. Some communities of Franciscan sisters have lay associate groups.

PRAYER

Lord, sometimes the temptation
to strike out on my own is very strong.
I can't see how my present life with my family,
or my brothers and sisters in community,
is allowing me to grow.
Everyone around me seems only a distraction or a burden,

and I wish I could just leave everything and everyone and be free.
But that is only a temptation most of the time, Lord.
For I find you in my commitments and responsibilities,
my loves and friendships,
not in fleeing them.
And in finding you, I find myself.
You are where I am, not somewhere else.
Lord Jesus, help me to discover you where I am.
Amen.

—Murray Bodo, *Tales of St. Francis*

REFLECTION (49)

A Rule for Keeping Order

The Seraphic Father Francis wished his ministers
to be courteous to their subjects, kindly and
gentle.... He wished them to be reasonable in
their commands, forgiving in the face of offenses,
more ready to bear than to return injuries, to be
enemies of sin but physicians of sinners. Finally
he wished them to be such that their lives would
be a mirror of disciplined living. On the other
hand, he wished them to be treated with all honor
and to be loved, seeing that they had to bear the
burden of cares and labors [cf. Matthew 20:12].

—Thomas of Celano, *The Life of St. Francis*

Francis himself had little knack for organization. He was a free
spirit, guided by the Spirit of God, drawing men to follow him
by the sheer force of his Gospel life. He thought of spirit rather
than law, the burning urgency of inspired Christians rather than
the more prosaic caution of experience. But he himself recognized
that thousands of Franciscans could no longer live according to
a few simple rules. Something was needed to keep some order in
the Franciscan household. Thus, Francis rewrote the Rule as the
situation demanded.

Francis wisely submitted his movement to the guidance of the
Church. The few Gospel texts that had been the foundation of the
early life of the Order gave way to more structure. Ideally, then
and now, structure helps all Franciscans contribute to the mission
of the Church.

At the core of the Christian life is Jesus Christ, manifested by the Body of Christ as he exists among his people. The Franciscan family is gathered by the Spirit as a body of people called together by God to live a Gospel life of prayer and service. It is a group of people who share a vision of the new life God calls them to, who care for each other in their needs, who form a place where God dwells, a joyous and prayerful people who are sent forth to build the Lord's kingdom.

A certain independence of thought and action is characteristic of the Franciscan way of life. Francis himself broke out of the medieval mold. But at the same time, Francis was in touch with the Holy Spirit and recognized the Holy Father as God's voice to him. In the Franciscan movement, there is a balance between independence and authority.

When we come to know Jesus as Francis did, we first need help. We are encouraged to look for it and to grow because of it. But there comes a time, when we need to reach out to help others. We will be thinking more of how we can help rather than what we can get out of it. Jesus and Francis gave their lives for the brothers and sisters. We can do no less.

The rules for the various orders of the Franciscans have a common thread that goes back to Francis's original vision, but they have been updated through the centuries to adapt to changing times. The current versions can be found online through a simple search. As you explore future directions for a Franciscan life, you might want to begin with the formal rule for the Secular Franciscan Order.

QUESTIONS FOR REFLECTION
- Why must a spiritual movement have structure?
- Is it possible for any movement to grow in numbers and variety of work without laws and organization?

CONNECTING WITH SCRIPTURE

The next day John again was standing with two of his disciples, and as he watched Jesus walk by, he exclaimed, "Look, here is the Lamb of God!" The two disciples heard him say this, and they followed Jesus. When Jesus turned and saw them following, he said to them, "What are you looking for?" They said to him, "Rabbi" (which translated means Teacher), "where are you staying?" He said to them, "Come and see." They came and saw where he was staying, and they remained with him that day. It was about four o'clock in the afternoon. One of the two who heard John speak and followed him was Andrew, Simon Peter's brother. He first found his brother Simon and said to him, "We have found the Messiah" (which is translated Anointed). He brought Simon to Jesus, who looked at him and said, "You are Simon son of John. You are to be called Cephas" (which is translated Peter).

—John 1:35–42

CONNECTING WITH FRANCISCAN WRITINGS

All who love the Lord with their whole heart, with their whole soul and mind, with all their strength (cf. Mark 12:30), and love their neighbors as themselves (cf. Matthew 22:39) and hate their bodies with their vices and sins, and receive the Body and Blood of our Lord Jesus Christ, and produce worthy fruits of penance.

Oh, how happy and blessed are these men and women because "the spirit of the Lord will rest upon them" (cf. Isaiah 11:2) and he will make "his home and dwelling among them" (cf. John 14:23), and they are the sons of the heavenly Father (cf. Matthew 5:45), whose works they do, and they are the spouses, brothers, and mothers of our Lord Jesus Christ (cf. Matthew 12:50).

We are spouses, when by the Holy Spirit the faithful soul is united with our Lord Jesus Christ, we are brothers to him when we fulfill "the will of the Father who is in heaven" (Matthew 12:50).

We are mothers, when we carry him in our heart and body (cf. 1 Corinthians 6:20) through divine love and a pure and sincere conscience; we give birth to him through a holy life which must give light to others by example (cf. Matthew 5:16).

Oh, how glorious it is to have a great and holy Father in Heaven! Oh how glorious it is to have such a beautiful and admirable Spouse, the Holy Paraclete!

Oh, how glorious it is to have such a Brother and such a Son, loved, beloved, humble, peaceful, sweet, lovable, and desirable above all: Our Lord Jesus Christ, who gave up his life for his sheep (cf. John 10:15).

—Rule of the Secular Franciscan Order, "Prologue: Exhortation of Saint Francis to the Brothers and Sisters in Penance"

APPLICATION TO DAILY LIFE

- Find ways to support others through sharing your faith and strength and reaching out to them.

PRAYER

Lord, thank you for the friends you have given me
along the way of my Christian journey.
May we support each other on our way to you.
Amen.

Following Francis in the Time of Pope Francis

During the election I had next to me the Emeritus Archbishop of São Paolo and Emeritus Prefect of the Congregation for the Clergy, Cardinal Claudio Hummes, a great friend, a great friend! When things began to look a bit dangerous, he gave me comfort. And when the votes rose to two-thirds, there was the usual applause, because the Pope had been elected. And he greeted me, he embraced me and he said to me, 'Don't forget the poor.' And those words lodged into me here [tapping his head]: the poor, the poor. Then, straight away, in connection with the poor, I thought of Francis of Assisi. Then, I thought about wars, while the voting continued until all the votes had been counted. And Francis was the man of peace. And so the name came to me, in my heart, Francis of Assisi. For me, he is the man of the poor, the man of peace, the man who loves and protects creation; at the present time, we don't have such a good relationship with creation, do we? He is the man who gives us this spirit of peace, this man of poverty.... Ah, how I would like a Church which is poor and for the poor.

—Pope Francis, speaking to journalists
after his election

There has been a resurgence of interest in St. Francis of Assisi and all things Franciscan since the election of Pope Francis. When this Jesuit cardinal took the name of Francis of Assisi, it set a tone for his papacy that brought new recognition to Franciscan themes, such as compassion for the poor and the outcast, humility, care for creation, peace and justice, and a simplicity of life. The pope's own lifestyle and activities have reflected these themes.

Like his namesake St. Francis of Assisi, Pope Francis has made joy one of the hallmarks of his papacy. It's a joy in the simple things in life and a focus on sharing God's love with everyone he meets. It's a way of looking at the world that sees hope and possibility, that emphasizes real connections over the distance that can accompany formality. His first apostolic exhortation was entitled The Joy of the Gospel.

For both Francis of Assisi and Pope Francis, the source of joy is a deep and abiding awareness of God's love for each and every one of us. If we trust that God loves us as individuals, as we are, we can't help but be filled with joy. If we know that we ourselves are loved, it becomes much easier to see that God loves those around us as well.

Francis of Assisi had a very clear understanding of the importance of the incarnation, of the Word of God becoming flesh in the person of Jesus of Nazareth. Because of this incarnation, all of creation was redeemed, restored to its original harmony with God. The more we let the word of God become part of our life, the more we will discover the joy that St. Francis experienced in living the Gospels. The more we conform our lives to the life of Christ, the more we will be moved by the presence and inspiration of the Holy Spirit.

Humility is another virtue Pope Francis shares with Francis of Assisi. His simple clothing choices, the Ford Fiesta that made such an impression when he visited the United States, and his choice to live in the St. Martha guesthouse rather than the papal apartments are some of the external signs of his commitment to a life of humble service. His motto is taken from a passage from the venerable Bede on the Feast of Matthew: *Vidit ergo Jesus publicanum, et quia miserando atque eligendo vidit, ait illi, "Sequere me."* [Jesus therefore sees the tax collector, and since he sees by having mercy and by choosing, he says to him, "follow me."]

His second encyclical, *Laudato Si*: "On Caring for our Common Home," takes its title from Francis's Canticle of the Creatures. Concern for the environment, stewardship of creation, and acknowledging the role of human sinfulness in the destruction that has taken place echoes the thoughts of the man who was named by Pope John Paul II as the patron saint of ecology.

Those who choose to live like Francis in the world have a shining role model in Pope Francis and will continue to be inspired by his challenge to live the joy of the Gospel.

CONNECTING WITH SCRIPTURE

As Jesus was walking along, he saw a man called Matthew sitting at the tax booth; and he said to him, "Follow me." And he got up and followed him.

And as he sat at dinner in the house, many tax-collectors and sinners came and were sitting with him and his disciples. When the Pharisees saw this, they said to his disciples, "Why does your teacher eat with tax-collectors and sinners?" But when he heard this, he said, "Those who are well have no need of a physician, but those who are sick. Go and learn what this means, 'I desire mercy, not sacrifice.' For I have come to call not the righteous but sinners."

—Matthew 9:9–13

CONNECTING WITH FRANCISCAN WRITINGS

I believe that Saint Francis is the example par excellence of care for the vulnerable and of an integral ecology lived out joyfully and authentically. He is the patron saint of all who study and work in the area of ecology, and he is also much loved by non-Christians. He was particularly concerned for God's creation and for the poor and outcast. He loved, and was deeply loved for his joy, his generous self-giving, his openheartedness. He was a mystic and a pilgrim who lived in simplicity and in wonderful harmony with God, with others, with nature and with himself. He shows us just how inseparable the bond is between concern for nature, justice for the poor, commitment to society, and interior peace.

Francis helps us to see that an integral ecology calls for openness to categories which transcend the language of mathematics and biology, and take us to the heart of what it is to be human. Just as happens when we fall in love with someone, whenever he would gaze at the sun, the moon or the smallest of animals, he burst into song, drawing all other creatures into his praise.... Such a conviction cannot be written off as naive romanticism, for it affects the choices which determine our behaviour. If we approach nature and the environment without this openness to awe and wonder, if we no longer speak the language of fraternity and beauty in our relationship with the world, our attitude will be that of masters, consumers, ruthless exploiters, unable to set limits on their immediate needs. By contrast, if we feel intimately united with all that exists, then sobriety and care will well up spontaneously. The poverty and austerity of Saint Francis were no mere veneer of asceticism, but something much more radical: a refusal to turn reality into an object simply to be used and controlled.

What is more, Saint Francis, faithful to Scripture, invites us to see nature as a magnificent book in which God speaks to us and grants us a glimpse of his infinite beauty and goodness. "Through the greatness and the beauty of creatures one comes to know by analogy their maker" (Wis 13:5); indeed, "his eternal power and divinity have been made known through his works since the creation of the world" (Rom 1:20). For this reason, Francis asked that part of the friary garden always be left untouched, so that wild flowers and herbs could grow there, and those who saw them could raise their minds to God, the Creator of such beauty. Rather than a problem to be solved, the world is a joyful mystery to be contemplated with gladness and praise.

—Pope Francis, *Laudato Si*

PRAYER

Most high, all-powerful, all good, Lord!
All praise is yours, all glory, all honor
And all blessing.
To you, alone, Most High, do they belong.
No mortal lips are worthy to pronounce your name.
All praise be yours, my Lord, through all that you have made,
And first my lord Brother Sun,
Who brings the day; and light you give to us through him.
How beautiful is he, how radiant in all his splendor!
Of you, Most High, he bears the likeness.
All praise be yours, my Lord, through Sister Moon and Stars;
In the heavens you have made them, bright
And precious and fair.
All praise be yours, my Lord, through Brothers Wind and Air,
And fair and stormy, all the weather's moods,
By which you cherish all that you have made.
All praise be yours, my Lord, through Sister Water,
So useful, lowly, precious and pure.
All praise be yours, my Lord, through Brother Fire,

Through whom you brighten up the night.
How beautiful is he, how gay! Full of power and strength.
All praise be yours, my Lord, through Sister Earth, our mother,
Who feeds us in her sovereignty and produces
Various fruits with colored flowers and herbs.
All praise be yours, my Lord, through those who grant pardon
For love of you; through those who endure Sickness and trial.
Happy those who endure in peace,
By you, Most High, they will be crowned.
All praise be yours, my Lord, through Sister Death,
From whose embrace no mortal can escape.
Woe to those who die in mortal sin!
Happy those She finds doing your will!
The second death can do no harm to them.
Praise and bless my Lord, and give him thanks,
And serve him with great humility.

—St. Francis of Assisi, *Canticle of the Creatures*

REFLECTION (5 1)

An Invitation

> "No one showed me what I had to do, but the Most High Himself revealed to me that I should live according to the pattern of the Holy Gospel."
> —St. Francis of Assisi, *The Testament*

Francis of Assisi, who was called the "little poor man," rediscovered the Gospel as a way of life. The Secular Franciscan Order is a community of men and women in the world who seek to pattern their lives after St. Francis of Assisi, and through him, Christ Jesus.

It has been in existence for over 750 years. Today, it includes over 700,000 members throughout the world. We invite you to join us. We believe that we have been called by the Spirit of God to live the Gospel, a vocation we cannot fulfill alone; we know we need other Christians, a community or fraternity that helps us in praying and serving others.

As St. Francis experienced a conversion of his life, so he leads us into a new world through a conversion experience. Each member is led through various steps of (1) looking over the Rule, (2) trying the Rule out through a program of prayer, study and action, and (3) making a "profession" of the Secular Franciscan Rule as their own way of life.

We are not called to leave the world, but to transform it. We remain in our families, maintain and deepen our friendships. But as we live our lives, our ideas, our prayer, and our lifestyle grow and change. The Spirit gives us light and power to transform and free us from all that hinders us from loving God and each other.

- We are brothers and sisters in a fraternity, expecting prayer and support from each other.
- We read and pray and live the Gospel to learn the ways of Christ.
- We are joined with Jesus and each other in the Eucharist.
- We are able to deepen our life of prayer and our union with God.
- We have special concern for the works of peace and reconciliation.
- We seek to live simply, value persons above possessions, sharing what we have with others.
- We strengthen our loyalty to the Church and her shepherds, as to the Lord.
- We strive to help the sick, the poor and the oppressed.
- We are able to develop leadership skills, receiving the gifts of the Lord with gratitude.
- We receive strength to overcome the difficulties of life.
- We receive healing from the Lord and each other.

QUESTIONS FOR REFLECTION

- Is the Franciscan way of life one you choose to follow all the days of your life?

CONNECTING WITH SCRIPTURE

After this the Lord appointed seventy others and sent them on ahead of him in pairs to every town and place where he himself intended to go. He said to them, "The harvest is plentiful, but the laborers are few; therefore ask the Lord of the harvest to send out laborers into his harvest. Go on your way. See, I am sending you out like lambs into the midst of wolves. Carry no purse, no bag, no sandals; and greet no one on the road. Whatever house you enter, first say, 'Peace to this house!' And if anyone is there who shares in peace, your peace will rest on that person; but if not, it will return to you. Remain in the same house, eating and drinking whatever they provide, for the laborer deserves to be paid. Do not move about from house to house. Whenever you enter a town and its people welcome you, eat what is set before you; cure the sick who are there, and say to them, 'The kingdom of God has come near to you.'"

—Luke 10:1–9

CONNECTING WITH FRANCISCAN WRITINGS

At every fork in the road, there was a narrow, difficult way and a wide, easy way to travel. And Francis was continually surprised with the paradoxical joy that the harder road would bring, time after time. Still, at every road the easier way attracted him with almost hypnotic persuasion. He never took the easy roads, not because he wanted to punish himself or the brothers, but because that is the way he read the Gospel. If Christ's words meant something else, then he was too ignorant to understand what that deeper, more hidden meaning was. He looked upon himself as a simple man from Umbria who expected words to mean what they said. That was all he was capable of.

And once he heard and understood the Word of God, he tried to put it into practice in his own life. For him the Word was life and not to live it was to deprive oneself of really living. That was what the Dream was all about in his own mind: to dare to live radically and simply, to take a chance on Christ. And what caused inestimable joy in Francis and his brothers was that the gospel worked. If you tried to live it without reservation, you suddenly experienced a whole new worldview, and you felt as though you had never lived before. Living became so precious that every moment was delicious and filled with the danger of risk and challenge, and the meaning of love came clear.

...

Francis prayed day and night that God would give all people the courage to be themselves instead of what others expected them to be.

He did not want everyone to enter the brotherhood or to join the Lady Clare and her sisters. He only wanted people to be free, to be what they wanted to be in their own hearts. For God spoke differently to each person, calling one to marriage, another to virginity; one to the city, another to the country; one to work with the mind, another with the hands. But who was brave enough to look inside and ask: "Is this what I should be doing, what I really want to do with my life?"

The Lady Clare left nobility to become a beggar, but his brother Pope Innocent remained Vicar of Christ's church. And both were totally free, really doing what they had decided they should do. Both were living their own lives and not someone else's. Who could do more?

—Murray Bodo, *Francis: The Journey and the Dream*

APPLICATION TO DAILY LIFE

- Reflect on where you have been in your life, how the Lord has been working. Admit your weaknesses and failures and trust in the power of the Lord to change you. Fear nothing and nobody.
- Give yourself to Jesus. Promise to work for him and his kingdom.

PRAYER

What way am I to go from this point in my life, Lord,
now that I know your faithful Francis better?
How am I to follow his way, your way?
Show me, Lord. Lead me, Lord. I am yours.
Amen.

REFLECTION (52)

Let Us Begin Again, and Again, and Again...

> "I have done what was mine to do; may the Lord
> teach you yours."
> —St. Francis of Assisi

The journey of the past year is a door through which you enter a new life—a life of the gospel, a life of the beatitudes. You are walking with the Lord in his life and in his way and in his truth. You can expect to be discouraged or frustrated or as the Bible says "in the desert" at times, but believe more and more strongly that Jesus is walking with you. He says, "Do not be afraid."

Francis came to know Jesus, and in doing so, he knew himself for the first time. Francis knew himself as the Poverello, "the little poor man," whose strength was in the Lord. He experienced the Lord working in his life. We need to do the same.

Know that the Lord is working in your life. Jesus says: "I will be with you." Difficulties, resentments, striving for power, and jealousies will crop up in your life and in the lives of your brothers and sisters. But Jesus doesn't abandon us; he stays with us, patiently comforting, guiding, and teaching, but also convicting us of sin and weakness. Jesus has a sense of urgency in the Gospel: "There is no time to lose. The life we live and the work we do is important for each of us and for his kingdom."

Strive to develop a deep life of prayer. Continue to set aside a period of time each day for prayer, both in praise of God and in intercession for your brothers and sisters. All of us are in need of the mercy of God.

Strive also to minister to others in your families and among your friends. The Lord calls us to be peacemakers, calls us to prayer to repair all the destruction which violence causes in the world. Reach out beyond yourself as Francis did. Reach out as Jesus did.

And finally, read the Word of the Lord every day, reflect on it, let it make a home in you. Make your daily decisions on the basis of what Jesus said and did. Believe that the Spirit continually calls us together to form the Body of Jesus today.

QUESTIONS FOR REFLECTION
• To what work is Jesus calling you?

CONNECTING WITH SCRIPTURE
This is my commandment, that you love one another as I have loved you. No one has greater love than this, to lay down one's life for one's friends. You are my friends if you do what I command you. I do not call you servants any longer, because the servant does not know what the master is doing; but I have called you friends, because I have made known to you everything that I have heard from my Father. You did not choose me but I chose you. And I appointed you to go and bear fruit, fruit that will last, so that the Father will give you whatever you ask him in my name. I am giving you these commands so that you may love one another.
—John 15:12–17

CONNECTING WITH FRANCISCAN WRITINGS
This new day. This song for beginning again. This harmony within me. This weightlessness I feel. Francis still caught glimpses from time to time of that first release, that beginning-anew feeling that filled his whole being the day he kissed the leper. The pent-up frustrations of his whole youth, the self-pity, the agonizing self-doubt and questioning, the moodiness of his illness—all rushed out of his heart as if a great dam had broken; and the backed-up, brackish waters of a lifetime streamed outdoors to be soaked up by the soil and forgotten forever.

That kiss, that reaching out of the lips directed his heart for the first time toward someone worth loving other than himself. He began that day to breathe out more than to breathe in, to turn outward rather than inward, to do rather than think about doing. He had finally found the courage to leap across that deep chasm that separated him from the other, from loving what he feared would demand more of him than he could give.

In keeping his eyes on the leper, in thinking only of this person before him, he forgot himself, he forgot the chasm beneath him, and he ran straight across the void into the arms of love and happiness. And all his life he struggled to preserve that original insight into love and to act it out daily. Love was looking into the eyes of the other; and forgetting the dark void between you and forgetting that no one can walk in a void, you start boldly across, your arms outstretched to give of yourself and to receive of the other.

In his last words to his brothers, his Testament, he said: "When I was in sin, it appeared too bitter to me to see lepers; and the Lord himself led me among them, and that which seemed bitter to me was changed for me into sweetness of soul and body." It was all there in those words: the walk to the leper was the Journey; what happened to you then was the Dream come true.

—Murray Bodo, *Francis: The Journey and the Dream*

APPLICATION TO DAILY LIFE

- Try to look at all those around you as brothers and sisters whom you love and cherish. Observe how this affects your view of the world.

PRAYER

Loving God, I give you honor, thanks and praise.
You forgive me when I fail to live according to the Gospel.

You encourage me when I do follow your way.
I ask for the faith and courage to begin again and again
to follow Jesus, my Lord and Savior.
Amen.

RESOURCES

Armstrong, Regis J., OFM Cap., and Ignatius Brady, OFM. *Francis and Clare: The Complete Works, Classics of Western Spirituality.* New York: Paulist, 1982.

Bach, Lester, OFM Cap. *The Franciscan Journey.* Secular Franciscan Order, 2010.

Bodo, Murray, OFM. *Francis: The Journey and the Dream.* Cincinnati: Franciscan Media, 2011.

———. *Francis and Jesus.* Cincinnati: Franciscan Media, 2012.

———. *The Way of St. Francis: The Challenge of Franciscan Spirituality for Everyone.* Cincinnati: St. Anthony Messenger Press, 1995.

Chesterton, G.K. *St. Francis of Assisi.* New York: George H. Doran, 1924.

Delio, Ilia. *Care for Creation: A Franciscan Spirituality of the Earth,* with Keith Douglass Warner, OFM, and Pamela Wood. Cincinnati: Franciscan Media, 2008.

———. *Clare of Assisi: A Heart Full of Love.* Cincinnati: Franciscan Media, 2007.

———. *Compassion: Living in the Spirit of St. Francis.* Cincinnati: Franciscan Media, 2011.

———. *Franciscan Prayer.* Cincinnati: Franciscan Media, 2004.

Englebert, Omer. *St. Francis of Assisi: A Biography.* Cincinnati: Servant, 2013.

Habig, Marion A., OFM, ed. *Secular Franciscan Companion.* Cincinnati: Franciscan Media, 1987.

———. *Saint Francis of Assisi: Omnibus of Sources.* Cincinnati: Franciscan Media, 2008.

Hutchinson, Gloria. *Six Ways to Pray from Six Great Saints.* Cincinnati: Franciscan Media, 2015.

Jorgensen, Johannes. *St. Francis of Assisi: A Biography*. London: Forgotten, 2015.

Kistner, Hilarion, OFM. *The Gospels According to Saint Francis*. Cincinnati: Franciscan Media, 2014.

Pope Francis. *The Spirit of Saint Francis: Inspiring Words from Pope Francis*. Cincinnati: Franciscan Media, 2015.

Rohr, Richard. *Eager to Love: The Alternative Way of Francis of Assisi*. Cincinnati: Franciscan Media, 2014.

Sweeney, Jon M. *When Saint Francis Saved the Church*. South Bend, IN: Ave Maria, 2014.

ABOUT THE AUTHORS

Jovian Weigel, OFM, was active with the secular Franciscans at local, regional, and national levels for more than thirty years.

Leonard Foley, OFM, was a popular retreat master and speaker on Catholic identity and Franciscan topics. He wrote the perennial bestseller *Believing in Jesus: A Popular Overview of the Catholic Faith*.

Diane M. Houdek, OFS, is digital editor at Franciscan Media and the author of *Lent with St. Francis, Advent with St. Francis, Pope Francis and Our Call to Joy* and *The Joy of Advent: Daily Reflections from Pope Francis*.